WORK
WITHOUT
STRESS

A Practical Guide to Emotional and Physical Well-being on the Job

Samuel H. Klarreich, Ph.D.

BRUNNER/MAZEL PUBL

Kasper, you will always remain a very
cherished memory.

Library of Congress Cataloging-in-Publication Data

Klarreich, Samuel H.
  [Stress solution]
  Work without stress : a practical guide to emotional and physical
well-being on the job / by Samuel H. Klarreich.
     p.   cm.
  Reprint. Originally published: The stress solution. Toronto, Ont.
: Key Porter Books, c1988.
  Includes bibliographical references.
  ISBN 0-87630-580-X. — ISBN 0-87630-579-6 (pbk.)
  1. Job stress. 2. Stress (Psychology) 3. Burn out (Psychology)
I. Title.
HF5548.85.K57   1990
158.7—dc20   90-30041
                                                          CIP

Published by
BRUNNER/MAZEL, INC.
19 Union Square West
New York, NY 10003

Paperback edition distributed to the trade by
PUBLISHERS GROUP WEST
4065 Hollis St., Emeryville, CA 94608
(800) 982-8319; in CA call collect 415-658-3453

Manufactured in the United States of America

10 9 8 7 6 5 4 3 2 1

Contents

I STRESS

Defining the Problem

Irrational Thinking

Consequences of Irrational Thinking

Stress Management by Counterthinking

II BURNOUT

Preface

What is counterthinking?

The word "counter" simply means opposing or acting in opposition to, as in "counteract," "counterattack," "counterbalance," "counterclockwise." Counterthinking, in essence, means thinking which is in opposition to previous thinking.

Why would this be a winning corporate strategy? It is a powerful approach because it offers a successful method of managing stress and burnout, the two ills of the corporate world.

Although, in recent years, many books have been written on the subject, more employees than ever before are suffering from stress and burnout. Why? First, because many of these books are not relevant to the workplace, and second, most of these books teach people to avoid or to become distracted from their problems, rather than to deal with them directly.

What is needed is a realistic and practical approach which gets at the root of these problems, that is, the harmful thinking that afflicts stress and burnout victims. That is what this book is all about.

Counterthinking procedures, or "cognitive" procedures, as they are referred to by health professionals, have been described by clinicians such as Drs. Richard Lazarus, Donald Meichenbaum, Cliff Christensen, Arnold Lazarus, and Aaron Beck, but none has been more influential than Dr. Albert Ellis. Dr. Ellis, who developed the Institute for Rational-Emotive Therapy (situated in New York), has written many books about the importance of thinking and beliefs to one's well-being. Books such as *A Guide to Personal Happiness; A New Guide to*

Rational Living; Executive Leadership and many others have contributed immensely to the field.

Over many years as a practicing psychologist, I have counseled individuals from junior ranks to the most senior, from a variety of businesses and industries. These people had their own sets of symptoms to describe and their own stories to tell. The demoralized secretary who felt so overburdened by the mess at work that she found one day that she could barely crawl out of bed to get into the office. The middle-level manager who was being sandwiched between her boss and the employees whom she supervised and who lost so much weight that she thought she was dying. The senior executive who lost his motivation to perform and wanted to quit the job he had worked twenty-five hard years to obtain. The frightened worker who, having just bought a new house and started a family, was so worried about losing his job that he almost killed himself in a car accident because he wasn't concentrating properly.

These histories, and many others like them, aren't meant to terrify you, but merely to point out how overpowering stress and burnout can be. But these people had one thing in common: they were helped. They came to grips with what was disturbing them, made the necessary changes and reestablished control over their working lives.

Over the years, I have not only counseled individual employees, but have also counseled companies on how to set up policies and programs to properly address these workplace hazards—stress and burnout. Yet this book will focus mainly on the individual employee in any given corporation, organization or business. Why? Although stress and burnout can tear apart the fabric of any organization, they first have to be experienced by the employees. In other words, if enough employees have these difficulties, their problems may eventually lead to the disruption and destruction of the company. It becomes very important, then, to examine the employees carefully and understand how these problems can do the damage.

My approach does not suggest that the organization as a whole should not be studied. Nor does it deny the fact that organizational culture, organizational climate and organizational stressors are real or valid factors. They are valid. However, for the purposes of this book, my focus will be on the individual.

Unlike many of the other books, this one will contain a strong intrapersonal and psychological perspective. Stress and burnout are, after all, emotional and psychological problems, and should be dealt with at that level. Too often, employees have been led to believe that if they get involved in "other activities," they will feel better, and their problems will disappear. This hardly ever works.

This book, unlike others before it, will teach you to develop strong thinking and reasoning skills as the best defense against stress and burnout. You will be taught to "counterthink." This is a very exciting possibility, because it will empower you to decide what "stinking thinking" got you in this mess to begin with, and what "counterthinking" procedures are needed to clear it up.

This book has a straightforward format. It offers practical techniques. It gives the reader the opportunity to think about a new and refreshing approach to problems which have plagued employees everywhere for time immemorial.

So enjoy the experience and learn something in the process.

Acknowledgments

I wish to heartily thank Dr. Albert Ellis, who opened my mind to the profound influence of "beliefs" and Rational Emotive Therapy; Dr. Cliff Christensen, who opened my mind to the power of "inferences and appraisals;" and you, Penny, who always inspire me to keep an open mind.

A very special thank you to Faustina Donson, whose typing wizardry was gratefully appreciated.

The author wishes to thank Praeger Publishers, a division of Greenwood Press Inc., for permission to use material adapted from the following articles:

S. H. Klarreich, "Stress: An Intrapersonal Approach," in *The Human Resources Management Handbook: Principles and Practice of Employee Assistance Programs,* ed. S. H. Klarreich, J. L. Francek and C. E. Moore (New York: Praeger Publishers, a division of Greenwood Press Inc., 1985). Copyright © 1985 by Praeger Publishers.

S. H. Klarreich, "Burnout—A Real Fire or False Alarm," in *Health and Fitness in the Workplace: Health Education in Business Organizations,* ed. S. H. Klarreich (New York: Praeger Publishers, a division of Greenwood Press Inc., 1987). Copyright © 1987 by Praeger Publishers.

I STRESS

Defining the Problem

Are You Overstressed?

These are some of the symptoms of stress:

- Increased heart rate
- Rapid breathing
- High blood pressure
- Stammering
- A tendency to withdraw and become isolated from colleagues
- Headaches, stomach aches, chest pains
- Reduced sexual drive
- Stomach and digestive disturbances
- Diarrhea
- Chronic fatigue
- Sweating
- Insomnia
- Accident-proneness
- Heart attack and stroke
- Ulcers
- Alcoholism and drug addiction

Some of these symptoms are mild, whereas some of the others are severe. You might ask, am I suffering from stress only if I have all or most of these symptoms? No, of course not. The most important thing is the *degree* to which you experience these symptoms. If you experience one of them very intensely, and over a long period of time, that might be as damaging as experiencing several over a short period of time. There is no single symptom of stress. What matters is how symptoms influence the way you function on the job and elsewhere in your life.

I have found that individuals often panic when they discover that they have developed the early symptoms of stress. They immediately draw hysterical conclusions: "Oh my gosh, I'm in trouble"; "I'm doomed"; "My productivity will collapse"; "I will never succeed on the job"; "Management will think I'm crazy"; "My career is kaput." When people indulge in such bizarre thoughts, their symptoms do not subside. If anything, they increase considerably.

Stress symptoms are not to be feared, but they do signal that you are not managing your life very effectively. They indicate that changes need to be made sooner or later, or more serious consequences may follow. They are warning you that you had better do something, and soon.

A human resources consultant who came to talk to me detailed what she went through each time she experienced stress symptoms:

"You know, I thought I was going to have a heart attack and die!

"I originally found out that I had stress when I complained to my family doctor about pains across my chest and feelings of dizziness. After visiting a number of specialists and going through a battery of tests, I was told that I had stress and that it would be important for me to learn how to relax. That's the last thing I needed to hear! I didn't believe them. I was sure that they had missed something. Every time I felt the chest pains and the dizziness, I thought that it was over.

"Eventually I realized that I was not about to die so quickly. Then I thought that I was definitely going crazy. I believed that I would slowly go to pieces, fall apart on the job, be carried out on a stretcher and watch my career go down the tubes. You know, all of this panic really did nothing for me, except make matters worse."

The Impact of Stress

You may have read about the billions of dollars that are probably lost each year as a result of stress. Stress is one of the most toxic of toxic agents encountered in the workplace. It can affect individuals at all levels of employment, in any organization. This includes members of the board as well as the maintenance staff. Stress can be triggered by a wide variety of situations which develop inside the organization as well as outside. We used to believe that if we were stressed at home, for example, we would experience some relief from the symptoms once we arrived at the workplace and started to do our jobs. Now we know that if we are stressed, we take it with us everywhere. If our family and marital life is unsatisfactory, it will affect us at work and everywhere else. If we are stressed on the job, we will drag our difficulties with us into the home.

According to some estimates, approximately 50 percent of all health-related problems can be attributed, in one form or another, to stress. As well, we know that stress manifests itself in a variety of destructive ways within any given organization. There is more illness and disability. There are more accidents and days lost due to absenteeism. There is an increased incidence of employee dissatisfaction. The quality of work declines. Projects are more likely to be delayed. Employees are more prone to impaired judgment and poor decisions. There is poor morale and a general malaise. In some instances, the failure to achieve corporate goals has also been linked to the level of stress prevalent in the organization.

Positive versus Negative Stress

Not all stress is negative or "bad." There is also "positive stress" or "good" stress, which I refer to as "arousal." Arousal is the kind of excitement, energy and enthusiasm that helps you with your performance, especially on the job. We all realize that in order to perform effectively, it is important to have a certain amount of energy and drive. If we did not have this arousal, we would appear lethargic, listless, "not with it"— simply out of touch with things.

"Negative" stress is simply overarousal. Negative stress or overstress, far from increasing efficiency, brings about a multitude of harmful consequences for personal health and well-being, as well as for on-the-job productivity. Feeling distressed or anxious definitely interferes with your ability to function.

Are You a Type A?
Ask yourself these questions:

Do you get bothered when you have to wait for something?

Do you find that you do everything quickly, such as eating, talking, walking, etc.?

Do you try to do a lot of things at one time?

Do you have a burning desire to be successful at everything you try?

Do you find that there is very little time to do all the things that you have to do?

Are you most comfortable when you are talking about what you are doing rather than what anyone else is doing?

Does your mind always wander when a person is conversing with you?

Do you define success as being able to do things faster, but not necessarily better, than your colleagues?

Do you believe that you and others are judged by performance alone?

Do you always find yourself competing with and trying to outdo those around you?

Are you constantly being told by those around you to slow down?

If you answered "yes" to many of these questions, you can probably consider your behavior to be "Type A." Some Type A behavior can predispose you to stress!

Origins of Type A Behavior

In the early 1950s, a cardiologist by the name of Dr. Meyer Friedman was carrying out investigations in the area of coronary heart disease. He observed that certain people with certain personalities and certain behaviors seemed to experience similar health problems. In essence, it seemed that particular individuals were more prone to heart disorders than other people were. Dr. Friedman subsequently collaborated with another cardiologist, Dr. Ray Rosenman. In their research, they coined the terms "Type A personality" and, later, "Type A behavior."

These two individuals drew our attention to the fact that the way people live ultimately influences their health. If people do things in a certain way, some of their actions may be detrimental to their health —perhaps so detrimental as to eventually contribute to heart problems. This conclusion was arrived at because the researchers observed repeatedly that people with various heart disorders had similar personalities and were behaving in similar ways. These early observations have contributed greatly not only to the field of Type A behavior, but also to that of health promotion and health education in the workplace.

This is the dawn of discovery. We are coming to realize more than ever before that the way we live and what we do with our lives, including our working lives, ultimately determines our health and our state of well-being. Furthermore, if we take certain precautions, we may be a lot happier and live longer.

As the two cardiologists continued their research, they eventually came up with a working definition of Type A. This definition includes the following: Type A behavior involves the feelings and actions of a person who is in a constant and urgent struggle to get a number of things from his or her workplace (or any other place, for that matter) in the least amount of time, and while doing this will challenge anyone who gets in the way.

The Healthy Type A

Between 50 and 60 percent of North Americans may be Type A, or at least demonstrate some Type A characteristics. The figure may appear high, but when you understand what Type A behavior is, you will begin to realize that many of us have felt and done some of the things that a typical Type A is engaged in.

Type As are usually driven to achieve and very competitive. In the effort to achieve, they come across in an aggressive, impatient manner. It is almost as if they are fighting time. They also seem to be struggling with themselves, with others and with the world and life in general. They seem to resent the world and people getting in their way. As a result, they come across as hostile, angry and resentful. This hostility and anger can flare up at almost any time.

You might ask yourself: "Who needs this?" Or: "Who would ever want to work with someone like this?" You'll be happy to know that this behavior is not contagious and that there is some good to being a Type A. To begin with, Type As usually strive to achieve a great deal. They push, drive and attempt to excel at every opportunity. They usually receive recognition for their efforts. There is usually a fair amount of social approval that comes their way from management and their supervisors. As well, they are rewarded for their achievements in a material sense. They may earn more money, and as a result have bigger homes, drive fancier cars and wear more expensive clothing. In social circles, they are typically lauded for their achievements. Others often marvel at their ambition and their level of accomplishment. Organizations and corporations have, over the years, grown to love Type As, because they get results. All this seems very good, and in fact it is good for Type As and for the organization, but there is a catch: the good news is eventually overwhelmed by bad.

The Anxious-aggressive Type A

Ask yourself these questions:

Do you feel agitated, uneasy and fidgety when you try to relax?

Do you feel on edge, jumpy and nervous when faced with tasks which need to be completed?

Do you find that you are bombarded by and obsessed with the many deadlines which are facing you?

Do you get rattled easily when things don't go your way?

Do you get incensed when policies and procedures stand in the way of your progress?

Do you find that you have no patience or tolerance for others who work more slowly than you do?

Do you believe that you carry the burden of responsibility for the success of your unit, department or organization?

Do you find that you often get angry?

Do you find that you speak loudly and on occasion swear in order to get your point across?

Do you find that you are regularly pounding a table or a desk, or waving a pencil or a ruler, in order to draw attention to what you are saying?

If you answered "yes" to many of these questions, you may be a candidate for stress.

Behavior and Stress

The Type A, as I mentioned earlier, is competitive. However, the anxious-aggressive Type A takes this competition just a bit too far. Ridiculously enough, he or she might even come up to you and shout: "Let's see who can get into work the earliest and leave the latest." These people are always struggling to outdo themselves and others at every turn.

These Type As are very involved in numbers. The number of their achievements becomes foremost in their minds. It is almost as if they are concerned about quantity and nothing else. Over time, quality suffers. They believe they are better simply because they do more. Is this really what organizations are looking for?

As these Type As continue on in their working lives, rushing around, making certain that they accomplish their daily quota, they get so caught up in numbers that they eventually become liabilities. They make decisions too quickly. They fail to consider long-range plans. They constantly explode at others who obstruct their short-term objectives. They eventually become pains-in-the-neck.

Inevitably, they find it difficult to work with others, because their colleagues are competitors who may eventually turn into the enemy. This type of unhealthy competition can only interfere with the Type As' work performance. Their solution is to isolate themselves. They find working with others a threat. When cooperation and teamwork are of utmost importance in business and industry today, how does this type of behavior fit into the picture? It doesn't!

Type As also have a tendency to hoard. They do not share any of their ideas or any of their work. This can be seriously counterproductive. These people do not delegate; they do not seek support and help. They grab every possible opportunity. They collect opportunities as others might collect toys. Eventually the work becomes unmanageable. There is simply too much to do and too little time in which to do it. This bad situation gets progressively worse.

I recall working with a manufacturing manager who described what his job was like. "It's a bloody rat race in that plant. You can't trust anybody. Some of those characters think they can get my job, but they never will. I can do more work than any two or three of those idiots. I don't share work with anyone. That's how I stay ahead, by working harder and longer. But I'll tell you, it's damn hard doing twenty things at once. I sometimes think I'm going crazy. But it's the only way I can survive in this madhouse!"

The Type As start to struggle to exert control over an increasingly uncontrollable set of demands. The more uncontrollable things become, the more the Type As try to control them. They find themselves becoming more exhausted and more frustrated, but they push on. They even begin to feel a sense of helplessness as the demands mount and the uncontrollable nature of the workload spirals. Because they are so afraid of failing and not completing tasks, they still push on.

Physical symptoms usually begin to occur. However, Type As don't pay attention to their symptoms, because they regard them as signs of failure and lack of control. Not only do they not report their symptoms, they pretend that the symptoms do not exist. They simply focus on the task at hand, making certain that they complete as much as they can in as little time as they can.

Because they do not pay attention to their symptoms, the symptoms usually get worse. If they did pay attention, they would realize that their lifestyle is inappropriate, and that their behavior needs to be changed. But instead, the mess continues to worsen.

The Type As become more and more dissatisfied with their work. They begin to feel a sense of personal failure. This, for the Type A, is a fate worse than death itself. This is when the bad turns into the ugly.

The relationships of the Type A begin to disintegrate. There are more quarrels at home. There is less time spent with spouses and children. Friendships are eliminated in favor of increasing hours on the job. Leisure activities are done away with. An appreciation of the simple pleasures in life is exchanged for escalated hours of desperation on the job. Type As begin to treat their spouses and children as if they are subordinates at work. They order them around. They shout at them. They expect them to fall into line. As a result, mutual support and understanding at home is simply abandoned. It gets worse.

These Type As now walk around with an abundance of hostility and irritability. They are easily frustrated and easily provoked to expressions of anger. It is as if they are always ready to do battle with any colleagues they encounter. Also, they rationalize their behavior. The world, and particularly the workplace, has been so bad to them that they in turn have to be bad to the world and the people they work with. They constantly legitimize their actions and carry on in an obnoxious fashion. They may also begin to consume more alcohol, smoke more cigarettes and generally abuse their health. They sleep less, they eat more irregularly, and they isolate themselves from key support people around them.

An advertising executive whom I saw explained his rut this way: "It got so bad that I hated myself and everyone around me. I hated my body because it let me down. I was getting dizzy, sweaty, short of breath. I was experiencing headaches, chest pains, stomach aches. But darn it, I figured that I would just work harder and it would go away. It never did.

"And those fools I worked with, I hated them as well. They got in the way of everything. They always told me that I looked bad, that I should slow down. What the heck did they know? They didn't know the pressure I was under. My family wasn't any better. They always wanted me to come home and spend more time with them. How the heck was I supposed to do that when I was always faced with at least half a dozen deadlines? The only safe hiding place was in my office, where I could be alone."

The Type A, after a time, begins to become a Jekyll and Hyde, growing unpredictable and moody and suffering from personality shifts. One day he or she may be very angry; the next, very depressed; and on the third day, very up and excited. When Type As are angry, they are angry at the world, the company, their family and their friends. When they are depressed, they are pessimistic, cynical, overburdened and over-whelmed. They are guilt-ridden. They blame themselves for every mess they have gotten into, and the mess everyone else has gotten into. They believe that they will never get out of their rut. On the other hand, when they are up, they can conquer the world. They can achieve it all. They can regain their success and accomplish what they always wanted to accomplish.

This does not happen to all Type As. But those who are considered chronic anxious-aggressive Type As usually end up in such a predicament. There is no question that all of us engage in Type A behavior in specific situations—but not throughout all of the situations which we experience from day to day. If you find yourself engaging in Type A behavior frequently and regularly, you have reason to be concerned about the quality of your life.

The Threat

Anxious-aggressive Type A behavior inflicts a lot of punishment on the body. There are many physical complications. People who are anxious-aggressive Type As usually exercise less, smoke more cigarettes, eat meals that are high in cholesterol and animal fat, and have more serum cholesterol and serum fat in their blood. This by itself can pose a health problem, but it is only part of the problem for Type As. There are other characteristics which, taken together, represent a serious risk of coronary heart disease.

As Type As do their thing in their own crazy fashion, whether it be at work or somewhere else, specific physical changes affect them. Because they are always running around as if they are chasing time, and are also anxious and angry, their bodies react by releasing hormones called adrenalin into the bloodstream. The heart rate, the blood pressure, and certain acids in the blood all increase. Once adrenalin increases in the bloodstream, it has been known to cause lesions, or small tears, in the inner lining of the arteries, particularly the coronary arteries. These are the arteries to the heart. If these arteries are weak to begin with, the lesions may ultimately cause severe heart problems. But the complications do not stop here. The same hormones have also been known to contribute to the formation of blood platelets. These blood platelets accumulate in the arteries and have been linked to *atherosclerosis* or "hardening of the arteries." Hardening of the arteries also contributes to heart disease. So, as Type As behave in their crazy way, they continue to produce adrenalin, which continues to work away at the arteries, causing damage to them, which in turn may ultimately cause damage to the heart.

A marketing representative who saw me for help recalled a terrifying experience. "I was always running in ten different directions, sometimes wondering what I was trying to accomplish. Anyone who got in my way really got a blast from me, boy! In fact, I fought with a lot of people I worked with, because they weren't on the ball and often made me look bad. While I was running around chasing time and quarreling with people, I just didn't feel right. I sometimes felt like I was going to pass out. One day, I had a heart attack at work! The ambulance came and they carried me out on a stretcher. That experience changed my life!"

Intense anger and hostility seem to be very important components of Type A behavior. They have been linked to coronary heart disease, high blood pressure and hypertension. Picture this angry and hostile person running around, talking quickly, exploding all over the place, shouting and throwing fits. It is not hard to see why this person, all of a sudden, would have an increase in heart rate and an accompanying increase in blood pressure. He would also probably begin to produce adrenalin, which could lead to permanent heart damage. Each and every time the Type A gets wound up, agitated, disturbed, suspicious and totally wrapped up in this anger and hostility, he may be putting his health at risk.

That is not to say that we should never get angry. We all get angry once in a while, and usually we get rid of the anger fairly quickly. However, intransigent Type As seem to experience anger for long periods of time, and the anger seems to be very intense. In a sense, they are driving themselves into the ground. By always increasing heart rate, blood pressure and the production of adrenalin in the bloodstream, they are repeatedly forcing their bodies into overdrive, when overdrive is not really needed. How much of this can the body take?

The other significant component, aside from anger and hostility, is the behavior called "time urgency," also labeled "hurry disease." This is the anxious side of Type A. Picture the Type A running around, trying to do twenty things at once, worrying about doing things too slowly, chasing time. She is obviously very impatient all the time. She is obsessed with speed and is trying frenetically to do more and more over a shorter period of time. She would probably experience the same bodily reaction associated with anger and hostility behavior. Again, the heart rate would go up, the blood pressure would rise, and probably those same hormones or adrenalin would enter the bloodstream. Again, this would present a serious risk to health. Whether the task is difficult or easy, Type As still run around as if they have had their heads cut off.

You can begin to appreciate how anger and time urgency can affect your system in general, and your heart in particular. Furthermore, I hope you now recognize why anxious-aggressive Type A behavior has been regarded as a serious health risk. Type As overmobilize their bodies. Whether they need to go into high gear or not, they have trained themselves to be frenzy machines. They could probably run a course on "How to do yourself in in no time at all."

Healthy and Unhealthy Type As

Not all Type As are on a course of self-destruction. There are some whose workload is really excessive, whose standards are too high, who are threatened too easily. They are unable to cope with the pressures and chaos around them. But this scenario is minor compared to the problems created by the two demons or "toxic components" of Type A behavior. Those Type As who are truly unhealthy and can be regarded as time bombs ready to go off are those who indulge in time urgency and anger and hostility.

Let me comment on a myth that is current in our society. It has to do with people who work excessively. We have often labeled such people "workaholics." Over the years workaholics have also been regarded as "time bombs." In fact, it is almost considered a sin to be a workaholic. But many workaholics lead very happy and successful lives, and are also very healthy. Workaholism is not a crime. It is not deleterious to your well-being. People who enjoy their work and are excited about it, who jump out of bed every morning looking forward to more, are generally very contented people. They also enjoy relationships with others and often engage in relationships with the same enthusiasm with which they engage in work. This makes for a very invigorating way of life. These are stimulating people to be around. Yet we devalue these people; we think that they are crazy. In fact, I think we envy their enthusiasm and energy.

A lawyer described her work schedule to me: "You know, I put in seventy to eighty hours of work each week. And I love it. I thoroughly enjoy what I do and the people I work with. I never get a cold or a sore throat, and I never miss work. When I went to visit my family doctor, she said I was as healthy as a horse. I feel great, enthusiastic and energetic. I have plenty of reserve energy for my family and my friends. And yes, they are very important parts of my life. I do run into occasional disagreements with my husband and kids about not being available for certain functions, but we usually iron out our differences, and as a result we understand ourselves better."

However, if workaholics were to engage in a constant expression of anger and time urgency, they would begin to experience the same symptoms and problems that we talked about earlier. This is when a happy workaholic turns into an unhappy, dissatisfied, stressed and ultimately burned-out individual.

Type B Behavior

Type B individuals have typically been described as having no driving urge or desire to succeed. They are people who do not have a strong need to accomplish. They can relax without feeling guilty. They seem to engage in activities with others for the enjoyment and pleasure of the experience, not necessarily to compete, to dominate or to drive the opposition into the ground. They seem to know what their limitations are, and they seem to be able to accept them. They seem to strive for what they want, but they do not go after it in such a frenzy or in such a hurry. They are also not overly sensitive to people's reactions. If they receive criticism, they usually take it reasonably well. They seem to be intelligent and ambitious, and they take time to think, to contemplate the future. They can examine short-term goals and think about long-term opportunities as well. They don't seem to be driven by the need to get results immediately.

They would seem on the surface to be individuals who are quite different from the anxious-aggressive Type As.

Questions, however, come to mind. Is a Type A at one extreme of behavior, and a Type B at the other extreme? What exists between the

Type A and the Type B? In answer to these queries, five categories have been developed. The first category is the fully developed Type A, who is the driven person we have been talking about. The second type is a moderately developed Type A. The third type is the moderately developed Type B. The fourth type is a fully developed Type B. Finally, the fifth type has a mixture of Type A and Type B behaviors.

Complicated? Yes, it is. Are there truly such distinct categories? No, I don't believe so. I believe that most of us are usually in the fifth category —sometimes we do things that can be classified as Type A and sometimes we do things that can be classed as Type B. So I don't think that we necessarily have to concern ourselves with the appropriate label. What is most important is what we do in certain situations. If we do things that are harmful to us in particular situations (especially indulging in the two most harmful behaviors, time urgency and anger and hostility), then we ought to try to correct that.

Stressors

"Stressors" are basically events, situations or changes, either in our work lives or our personal lives. A great deal has been written about the variety of changes that can produce stress. Many of us have been convinced that the more change we experience, the more we will be stressed. Some individuals have become so worried that they begin to think, "My gosh, I'd better not experience any more changes, otherwise I'll be stressed to the point where I'll crack up." Perhaps few of us go so far, but it is critical to realize that stress is not simply caused by changes.

However, there are people who have invested a lot of energy and a lot of time listing all sorts of events which they regard as stress producers. Such events in the workplace include:

- Being fired
- Being in competition with a colleague

- The death of a colleague or associate
- A demotion
- Being transferred to another division or to another part of the country
- Starting a new job
- A decrease in your income
- A conflict with a colleague or supervisor
- Being overqualified for your job
- Being underqualified for your job
- Having to deal with people who are aggressive
- Noisy environment
- Uncommunicative colleagues or supervisors

There are many more. But the sources of stress do not stop here. Many events which occur in our everyday lives outside of work have been described as causing stress, including:

- The death of a spouse or family member
- Separation, divorce, marriage
- The shock, or trauma, of natural disasters
- Difficulties with in-laws
- Moving to a new neighborhood
- Sale of a house
- Purchase of a house
- Vacation
- Christmas

If we were to believe that all of the above life changes cause stress, then we would virtually have to stop living to avoid stress. Changes are important, but they do not necessarily cause stress. If they did, then everyone who experienced these changes would experience the same degree of stress.

Consider divorce, which has often been referred to as a major stressor. We know that four or five marriages out of every ten end in divorce. It would seem to follow that a lot of people are, sooner or later, going to be extremely disturbed and have their lives greatly disrupted. But this is not the case. There are people who are delighted to be divorced. Some men and women view it as a positive change, a step forward. In fact, a Toronto college even offered a course entitled "Creative Divorce." The originator of the program took the view that divorce is the first step to a new and enriched life.

The president of a union spoke to me about his divorce. "I thought I would be completely shattered, but, to my surprise, I wasn't. I realized that my wife and I were both unhappy and we simply weren't able to live together anymore. You know, we actually get along better now that we are divorced. In fact, we go out together once in a while and we truly enjoy each other's company. Divorce has been a godsend for both of us."

Being fired is a critical stressor for a lot of people. Here again, we assume that anyone who is fired experiences tremendous anxiety and discomfort. But again, this is not necessarily so. There are some people who are almost delighted to be dismissed. This is not to say that we should all go out of our way to get fired. It simply means that some people view this stressor differently. They think things through and come to the following conclusions: they are going to receive a good severance arrangement; they have an opportunity to explore exciting new options; they are leaving an environment which is too uncompromising; they will be able to work with different, maybe more exciting, individuals; they will have new opportunities for advancement; and they will simply be happier now that they are no longer a member of a team which they never really felt part of.

I remember talking to an administrator who, in the course of a year, left one job and started another, sold his house and bought another, and went through a divorce. In addition, an important member of his family passed away, and his daughter suffered a serious illness. You might suppose that this man must have gone crazy because of the stress he experienced. In fact, he indicated that he was never healthier than he was during this period. There was so much going on, and he was spending so much energy in managing all these changes, that he felt healthier and more vibrant than he ever had before.

Let me give you another example: a death, especially the death of a spouse. I think we would all agree that this is a major event in our lives. Many people would state categorically that this event inevitably brings on stress. But this is not necessarily true. There have been people who have found that when their spouse has been buried, they can begin to live again. They view it almost as an inspiration. One man told me: "My wife was in pain. Thank God she has passed away." Another client said: "I was going through tremendous pain while my husband was suffering. Now I feel such relief. I know he has now passed on to a more serene and beautiful place."

How you perceive an apparently stressful event is the critical factor. In some cultures death is viewed as another step toward a life hereafter. Death is seen as a wonderful experience, a transition. In these cultures, stress would be the last reaction to death that any member would experience.

Let us look at robbery as a stressor. I think that we would all agree that being the victim of a robbery is a very critical experience. Again, we might assume that anyone who has gone through it would be extremely upset for a long time. However, that is not accurate; robbery is not stressful in the same way for all victims. Some victims seem to suffer the symptoms of stress more than other victims because of the way in which they view the event. Some victims view the robbery experience as devastating, and say to themselves: "I cannot stand this anymore;" "I hate people;" "I am never going to be able to survive this;" "My home is ruined forever;" "I will never be able to feel comfortable in this house again;" "I am going to be depressed for the rest of my life;" "I hate everybody because of how destructive they are;" "There is no way that I can ever sleep here for fear that it will happen again." If you were to view robbery in this fashion, you would have no choice but to be stressed. That is not to say that robbery as an event is not significant. It is. But you do not necessarily have to be severely and chronically disturbed by it. Other victims, who apparently are less distressed and disturbed, view robbery in a different way. They say to themselves: "This is not the end of the world;" "If I'm lucky this will never happen to me again;" "My home was burglarized but not destroyed;" "Items were stolen but most can be replaced. Those important possessions which can't be replaced, I will cherish in my memory." It is these views that are important. This perspective tends to minimize stress, no matter what stressor occurs.

A very significant stressor is trauma. Let us take the example of a major disaster, say a hurricane or a tornado which has just wiped out a community. Most people would assume that if you had your home and everything inside it destroyed, you would be devastated, and that any-one who experiences such a shock and lives to talk about it should be physically and psychologically ruined. But again, people do not always react in the same way, and thus do not experience the same degree of stress. Indeed, some people seem to cope with disaster reasonably well. Their perception makes the difference. A person likely to be extremely disturbed and bothered might think the following: "I will never get over this; I will never be able to go on. God was rotten to me." Another might think: "The world is evil and everyone in it is evil." Or: "Why did this have to happen to me and my family? I will never be able to get back on my feet." Or: "I am going to be miserable for the rest of my life. How will I ever continue? I am ruined."

But there are some people who perceive things differently. As a result, the amount of disturbance which they endure is significantly reduced. I don't intend to deprecate the importance of this event or stressor. What I am emphasizing is the importance of your outlook. Individuals whose distress would be minimized might think the following: "The fact that my home is ruined does not mean that my life is ruined." "I have my health, my family has their health, and we can go on." "If I built it up once, I can build it up again." "Not only can I survive, but I am looking forward to the challenge." "A challenge like this will bring our family together." "If we can survive this, we can survive anything."

We need not be controlled by the changes in our lives. The fact that we encounter stressors and changes does not mean that we are destined to suffer stress. Many of us have been brainwashed to believe that we are victims. We are convinced that we are slaves of our environment. Type As, in particular, are convinced that they are victims. Type As go around dramatizing, "catastrophizing," talking doom and gloom. Their perspective is warped.

It may appear that I am recommending positive thinking: "Just follow the message of this book and everything will be wonderful! Think positive and your problems will be solved!" In fact, I am not necessarily endorsing positive thinking, but I am recommending the adoption of a realistic view. A perspective that is based on what you are faced with, here and now, is the starting point. A sensible, logical, even optimistic outlook can turn things around. If you have the choice either to experience stress, or not to, which would you choose? Of course, you would choose not to experience these symptoms. And the choice *is* yours! You can maximize or minimize your unhealthy reactions by paying attention to your outlook. It is your thinking that makes an event stressful for you.

But remember this: You are entitled to feel concern, you are entitled to feel upset, you are entitled to mourn and to grieve for your losses. These reactions are human and natural. Such normal reactions do not, however, have to result in chronic or severe stress.

Does the Organization Cause Stress?
We have all become very sensitive to events within organizations. We

often believe that situations in the work environment produce our problems. While I do not rule out the importance of organizational factors, I believe that we can largely determine what will be stressful, and how much it will interfere with our lives, by the views we uphold, irrespective of what goes on in the workplace. Some specialists in human resources, organizational development and organizational effectiveness might take issue with this. But it seems to me that if conditions within the organization caused all stress, then all employees in that environment would suffer in the same degree, at the same time. And this just does not happen. Certain employees think one way and experience difficulties, while other employees think another way and undergo minimal discomfort. So to say that the company is "doing us in" is incorrect. We do ourselves in. There may be certain work conditions which require change, but this is a separate issue. In order to reduce their distress employees must first examine what is going on inside their heads. Then they can take a look at their particular work environment, and decide what changes to go for.

A data processing manager whom I helped discussed his philosophy: "I always blamed the company for my problems. Because I had so many meetings to attend, so many deadlines to meet, so many outdated policies to contend with, so many hassles from my client groups to handle, I was always nervous, tense and irritable. If only the company would be more sensitive to my needs and make my life a little bit easier, I was sure I'd feel a lot better. But one day I looked around at other managers. Some of them seemed to be handling matters quite well. They had the same hassles I did, yet they weren't as uptight. After talking to them, I found out that their thinking was different. They didn't take things so seriously, and therefore the everyday problems didn't get to them as much. Then I realized that maybe I was the problem. Perhaps I was just too worried about too many things. That's not to say that my company is perfect! But maybe I was too demanding both of myself and of those around me. I'll tell you, once I stopped driving myself crazy, I got more work done. Also, I was able to change some of the things which bugged me, because people finally listened to me and stopped seeing me as a royal pain in the behind."

Definition of Stress

Stress is a non-specific physiological and psychological response to events which are perceived as a threat to one's well-being, and are thus handled ineffectively.

In simple terms, stress is made up of symptoms which occur as a result of events or situations, which in the workplace may involve colleagues, supervisors, workloads, and so on, that you perceive as a threat to your health. Because you hold this view, the events are typically managed very poorly.

The key element in this definition is what you as an individual regard as a threat to your health and well-being.

Irrational Thinking

Always Thinking

Whether we realize it or not, we are all thinkers. In fact, it would be safe to say that we think chronically. Each and every day, whether we are aware of it or not, we ponder something or other. As human beings, we think in many different ways. Sometimes we talk to ourselves and reflect in words, phrases and sentences. At other times we visualize certain images and think to ourselves in pictures, fantasies and dreams. Often, after we have thought about what has happened at work or at home, we tend to rehearse what we should have done or said and how we should have felt.

Being human, we have a tendency to think rationally, realistically and reasonably—but we also have a tendency to think irrationally, unrealistically and unreasonably.

If we proceed to think irrationally, unrealistically and unreasonably, we are likely to experience a variety of harmful feelings and symptoms that include anxiety, worry, fear, anger and depression, which are stressful. On the other hand, if we choose to think rationally, reasonably and realistically, we will probably experience more helpful and comfortable feelings, such as concern, compassion, sorrow, love, joy, happiness and contentment, which are not stressful.

We have a choice. We can choose to think in nonsensical terms or in sensible terms. Once we make that choice, it will largely determine how we feel. If we feel stressed, we can assume that our heads are filled with unsound, absurd, ridiculous nonsense!

To complicate matters further, we sometimes think about the way in which we think. If we think irrationally and unreasonably and bring on stress, we begin to worry about the crazy ideas that are running through our heads. We then upset ourselves more, and create even more stress, by thinking that we are crazy for the way in which we are thinking. Complicated, yes!

Thinking and Doing

Our society is very big on *not* thinking. We are very big on doing. In almost every major organization and corporation, the emphasis is on getting the job done. The emphasis is on problem solving, on completing tasks. Action is seen as the first and foremost activity. Thinking is secondary.

Dr. Edward De Bono, who created the concept of "lateral thinking," has pointed out that "our conceptual area is the critical area." He has stated that "the quality of our future is going to be designed by the quality of our thinking."

Organizations and industries around the world would benefit tremendously if they encouraged more thinking. Problem solving should be secondary to thinking.

Under the circumstances, it is not surprising that many employees are struggling with stress. They are encouraged to solve the problem quickly and get it out of the way: "If you have a problem with stress, do something about it! Get your life in order and get on with it!" But how can employees be expected to get on with managing their lives, unless they think about it first?

"Fight or Flight"

When we were cavemen and cavewomen, we must often have found ourselves in a position where we needed to fight in order to preserve our lives. We could be attacked at any time by all sorts of interesting creatures. We had to be always ready for combat. Our bodies prepared us by releasing certain hormones into the bloodstream as required. These "nerve hormones" or adrenalin caused the heart to react. The muscles would then respond, the stomach would be prepared—our bodies were ready for battle.

When we chose not to do battle, but were scared, we would run. The body would prepare itself in the same way. The brain, the heart, the stomach, the muscles, were all ready for running.

As employees today, we often react to problems as we used to when we were cavemen and cavewomen—as if our very lives are being threatened. We fight or run! This reaction makes sense if we are attacked by animals that could kill us. But in the workplace, wild animals are not likely to attack. Yet certain employees seem to think such a threat exists. They view their colleagues as animals, and their supervisors and managers as creatures from some black lagoon! And they react physically to the perception, as if the threat were real, by preparing themselves to fight or flee. These employees repeatedly put extraordinary pressure on themselves and their bodies. Their faulty perception of their situation makes them become victims of stress.

Sixteen Irrational Thoughts

Illogical thinking is what manufactures stress. Normal events in the workplace are transformed by our thinking into threatening situations which can become hazardous to our well-being.

There are two main categories of events which give us grief. One group relates to tasks, projects and assignments—in general, to work. The other group relates to colleagues and managers—in general, to people. People's thinking about these events involves a great deal of worrying, agonizing and "catastrophizing." People are plagued with panic about some possible disaster which may be waiting for them around the corner. What follows is a variety of panic-laden thoughts about the two categories of events in the workplace—thoughts which get us into trouble.

1. Something terrible will happen to me if I make a mistake.

In this case, the employee is terrified of making an error. He is convinced that he is going to be criticized by his manager. He worries that he may be fired. He dwells on, ruminates about, ponders the terrible things which are bound to happen if he makes a mistake. Is this reasonable? Is it realistic? Of course not! But many employees spend a lot of time worrying about making errors. They became so fearful that sometimes they stop performing altogether.

2. There is a right and a wrong way to do things.

It is obviously right to succeed and be a sensation on the job. It is equally obviously wrong to fail, because something awful will happen. Work is usually not a simple matter of success or failure, but there are hordes of employees who have this black-and-white view of the work world. And they constantly feel threatened when things aren't correct, whatever "correct" really means. If something was truly "right," then we would all be doing the "right" thing. But certain employees behave as if there exists a true right and drive themselves crazy trying to achieve it.

3. It is awful and horrible to be criticized.

The employee who thinks this thought is convinced that if she is criticized, she must be a failure in the eyes of management. What's more, her colleagues must think that she is incompetent, too. And once she has been put down, she will never be able to recover. Type As constantly fear severe reactions from others. Criticism is a common feature of the working day, and sometimes it may be destructive rather than constructive. But it is not reasonable to fear all criticism like the plague.

4. I must be approved of, all the time.
Certain employees have a strong need for positive feedback. They pray that management will tell them that they are doing a great job, because then they can feel like winners, and walk with their heads held high for everyone to see.

All of us would like to receive positive feedback and commendation, but is it so awful if we don't get it? Yet certain employees feel that they can't go on without their regular dose.

5. I must be competent, and especially be viewed that way.
This person demands that management rate him extremely highly, and that his colleagues tell him that his performance is extraordinary.

What if this does not occur? Does it mean that the person has failed? Does it mean that he will never amount to anything in the organization? Some employees really believe that this is the case and worry about it.

6. People in authority should never be challenged.
In other words, if I disagree with my supervisor I will probably be fired. Or, if I have a debate with a colleague, he will think I am a terrible person to work with and have nothing to do with me. Certain employees take on a multitude of jobs, even though they are overworked, simply because they are afraid to say no. If they do say no, it might cause some disagreement. If it causes some disagreement, they may not receive approval; they might not be viewed as competent; and they might be identified as troublemakers.

Surely this is a bit far-fetched! No employee can hope to cooperate fully with everyone around her 100 percent of the time. She sometimes has to challenge what her supervisor and colleagues say and do.

There has been some intriguing research in the area of cooperative relationships, particularly friendships. It appears to be the case that the most trusted friends are those who agree with us sometimes, but disagree with us at other times. In other words, we appreciate honesty in thought and expression of feeling more than we appreciate mere passive agreement. However, when there is constant agreement or constant disagreement, there is friction. If you are constantly disagreeable, obviously you are going to have trouble forming any kind of relationship, let alone friendships. On the other hand, if you constantly go out of your way to say "Yes, I agree," other people will not trust your judgment or fully accept your friendship.

Now, apply this principle to the workplace: you are a typical employee who always says "yes," "I will do this," "I will do that." What happens? Some colleagues and managers are simply not going to trust you.

Clearly, it is not in your best interest to be always agreeable. At times you should disagree, not for the sake of disagreeing, but to voice your difference of opinion and thought. Your working relationships will be more meaningful as a result.

7. Life in the workplace must be fair and just.
What does "fair and just" really mean? For the Type A individual it means that management should listen to what she says. And furthermore, her colleagues should agree with what she says. After all, she is the expert; she knows what she is doing. How realistic are thoughts like these? Well, certain employees believe that if they are not treated in this fashion, they will be unable to tolerate it. If they don't receive justice by their reckoning, they will feel insecure, ill at ease and threatened. It becomes very difficult for them to get any work done.

8. I must be in control all of the time.
Otherwise I'll amount to nothing. The employee who thinks this thought has to be continually bright and alert. He thinks that he must respond brilliantly, especially in the presence of management, to every situation that arises. He feels that once he comes across in this magnificent fashion, he will acquire all the positive feedback he desires, and will always be viewed as competent and capable.

If he doesn't receive this feedback, who knows what terrible things will happen to him? But is it possible to be right and alert all the time? Of course not. Yet certain employees feel that this is their mandate in life. How else will they shine and achieve their goals? Their peers and supervisors must regard them as supreme beings. Clearly, this is another line of thinking that can get you into trouble and generate a lot of panic!

9. I must anticipate everything.
Otherwise I'll never get ahead. This idea contains others, such as: "I must know what is going on in my manager's head;" and "I must be prepared to handle everything and anything that my colleagues dish out." Certain employees pride themselves on being able to read everybody's vibrations. They would like to think that they have the power to second-guess people all of the time, that they can always stay one step ahead of them. Then, and only then, will they be able to win in their competition for success and glory.

I'm a psychologist. I'm supposed to be able to read people's minds, but I'm not very good at it. But Type As are convinced that they can read vibrations and more or less predict what people will say and do. This makes no sense, but try to persuade a Type A that it doesn't! Furthermore, once a Type A guesses incorrectly, just try to convince her that her judgment is faulty, especially if she believes her career is on the line. You'll have a full-blown battle on your hands!

10. I must have things the way I want them.
If I don't, that proves to the world that I haven't made it. This really means: "I must have a prestigious position, a beautiful office and a fantastic salary." Certain Type A employees are convinced that this line of thinking makes sense. When the things they want do not materialize, they believe that somehow they have failed themselves and those around them. Many become angry when they don't get what they feel they deserve. After all, they have pushed, they have striven, they have driven for success.

Again, you are setting yourself up for tremendous disappointment by subscribing to these unreasonable thoughts. Yet Type As do not think that their ideas are unrealistic. And, when their demands are not fulfilled, their world caves in around them.

11. Employees who are wrong should be punished.

If they are not, the organization will surely collapse. Certain employees are intolerant of people around them, especially colleagues who make mistakes. At the same time, they are worried that the company will go under if justice isn't meted out. Such a person may think that if a fellow employee makes a mistake, he should be demoted. Of course, the intolerant employee, being an outstanding employee, should be promoted in the other's place. And she thinks, furthermore, that if management does not promote her, and does not demote that incompetent whom she works with, then the manager should be taken to task. This attitude may seem extraordinary, but certain employees place themselves above everybody else, and are angry when the others are not doing things right. They have very high standards. They really think that others who don't live up to their standards should be punished. They pride themselves on their ability to determine who should be admonished and who should not.

No wonder these people have difficulty getting along with their colleagues! They are convinced that they know everything: they know what is right; they know what is wrong. If others do not measure up, then they should be doomed to failure.

Isn't this grossly unrealistic? If you stroll around your department with these thoughts in mind, you are setting yourself up for trouble. You are bound to become alienated from your colleagues. Your job performance will be adversely affected. Ultimately, you are putting yourself under unbearable pressure and will suffer at least some of the symptoms of stress as the result.

A senior stockbroker talked to me about a problem he had: "I always walked around as if I had a chip on my shoulder. I knew everything. I couldn't be bothered talking to the people I worked with, because they were a waste of time. After a while, I began to realize that I didn't have anyone to talk to. I had become so used to avoiding people that now people were avoiding me. I started to get down on myself and I noticed that my work started to slip. It's hard coming in to work every day and being totally alone and isolated. But I guess I created this mess."

12. I must have somebody's shoulder to cry on.
The person who thinks this thought feels that he can't get out of a work-related problem without the total support of his colleagues. He also needs to have management feel sorry for him.

Typically, when this individual gets into a tough spot, he expects the world to react immediately. He expects his working group to comfort, reassure and sympathize with him. He is terrified that the pressure will be too much and that he will cave in. To prevent a collapse, he must be bolstered by people in the work environment. If he obtains the support he craves, it proves to him that he will make it after all. This reasoning is pretty far-fetched. No doubt it is nice to have people nurture you when you feel down. But what if they don't? What if you do not receive the understanding and consideration which you demand? There is no reason to believe that you are going to come apart at the seams, though the conviction may become a self-fulfilling prophecy.

13. I must feel perfect all the time.
Otherwise I'll never succeed. Not some of the time, or even most of the time, but all the time! Feeling perfect, when you think about it, is a complicated idea. Certain employees believe that they must not feel nervous or anxious, or get discouraged or down. They think that everybody should be up; everybody should be with it; everybody should be smiling and completely happy. Successful people never get discouraged, or down, or nervous or jumpy. People who do experience any of these negative feelings have failed.

Talk about a heavy load to carry! There are times when everyone feels uncomfortable. There are times when everyone feels down. It's only normal and human to experience a wide variety of feelings. Our emotions may range from ecstasy and joy to feelings of discouragement, discomfort and nervousness. No one can feel perfect all the time.

14. My worth as a person is exactly equated to my job performance.
I'd better perform extraordinarily well—otherwise who can tell what unfortunate fate will befall me? This thought is critical. It is the one premise that pervades the mind of every Type A walking the corporate corridors.

Many employees mistakenly believe that who they are is determined by what they do in the workplace. If such an employee performs well on the job, he will probably think to himself that he is a wonderful human being, a tremendous performer and an asset to the firm. Should he not execute his job well, however, he will persuade himself that he is no good, incompetent, worthless and an outright failure. No wonder his feelings go up and down like a yo-yo!

The Type A individual is bound to think that she, or anyone, must be a real idiot to blow a project or bomb out on a particular job. Of course, she isn't. If she doesn't do well at something, it simply means that she hasn't done well! There is no reason for her to condemn herself.

Certain employees, Type As in particular, generalize. They think that because they failed on the job, they will perform inadequately everywhere. In other words, having been a lousy employee, they will be lousy parents, contemptible spouses or a combination of both. They will conduct themselves amateurishly in the social arena. They will be careless listeners, miserable friends and social misfits. What's more, they will be inferior lovers and not measure up in bed. Because they did not meet their own high standards on the job, they expect never to do anything well again.

Of course, this line of reasoning is ridiculous! But this is the way certain people think and so consign themselves to a private purgatory.

15. I was promised a corporate rose garden.
This thought implies that work and activities on the job must always be rewarding and satisfying. As the individual continues to carry out her

responsibilities, management must be considerate toward her. Management must be kind and show her respect. If she doesn't receive what's coming to her, she won't stand for it. This is what a corporate rose garden is all about. After all, why would this person go to work, unless it was completely gratifying and everyone treated her with courtesy and admiration? Again, I submit that this thought does not make sense. There are, however, a number of people who parade around the workplace thoroughly convinced that this is the way things should be—and if they are not, watch out! It is almost as if there are well-formulated rules carved in stone about the way working conditions should be arranged and the way people should behave. It would be great if one's job was completely rewarding and satisfying. It would be equally gratifying if, once we offered our opinions, everyone perked up, showed some respect for our views and even acted on the basis of our advice. But it's not going to happen very often.

16. It is too late for me to change, and if you expect it, I won't be able to handle it.
In this case, the employee makes it very clear that he is determined to stay the way he is. He is unable to make any meaningful changes, because he read somewhere that after the age of twenty-one people are no longer capable of change.

Characters like this do exist. They make it quite clear to their managers and their colleagues that they plan to behave in the same rigid and uncompromising fashion, and that people around them will have to accept this. They have further persuaded themselves to believe that their ill-conceived actions are part of their personalities and can never be altered. Finally, they are convinced that because their behavior contributed to their success in the past, it must be upheld now, even though they may be having problems with work, with management and so on. Also, they are afraid to change because they might fail if they try something new.

These employees are unbending in their determination to remain the same. When they receive an unsatisfactory performance review, they are likely to quit, saying that management is crazy. They will not accept that what they are doing is wrong or inappropriate. At most, they may concede that their methods have not been applied with enough thoroughness or enthusiasm. They are certain that, sooner or later, their old formula will regain for them the success which they desperately crave. So these employees continue in their misguided ways and will not change, no matter what. There are lots of these characters around. And they repeatedly get themselves into trouble because of their pigheaded, panic-ridden thinking.

I recall speaking to a financial analyst who really hurt her career with her stubborn approach. "I always believed that I was right and that I never had to change. Because I experienced success early in my career, I thought that I had the magic formula for success—my way or nothing. I knew that I was bright. I scored at the top every year at university and I was voted by my graduating class as the one most likely to succeed. When I first joined the company, I impressed everyone immediately. I was pegged as a 'fast-tracker,' a 'water-walker.' I had all 'the right stuff.' My decisions were impeccable.

"But when I moved into the ranks of management, my problems started. I didn't seem to be able to manage people well. I only expected from them what I expected from myself—nothing less than perfection. I was repeatedly warned about my demanding, authoritarian approach. Many times, I was asked to change my management style. However, I was convinced that it was my staff's fault. If they would only do what I told them, everything would be fine. And what the heck did my own manager know? She had been with the company too long, and her ideas were outdated. She didn't have half the talent or brainpower I had. So I stuck to my guns, because I knew that I was right, and also because I was fearful to find out that I might be wrong. Until, one fateful afternoon, I was asked to leave the company."

Consequences of Irrational Thinking

Dumb Behavior

We have spent considerable time talking about some of the irrational thinking that we can engage in. And we now know that if the thinking is worrisome enough, it sets the stage for a lot of bodily reactions, which we label as stress. But irrational thinking not only leads to uncomfortable feelings; it also prepares us for some dumb actions, that is, actions which do not achieve any meaningful results.

We know that corporations and organizations, in all sectors of industry, emphasize efficiency. Business today is interested in the bottom line and in results. To achieve ambitious goals, to reach targets, to accomplish the corporate mission statement, employees need to work together, to cooperate, to work as a team toward the common good. On a more personal level, employees who wish to achieve specific career objectives realize that it is imperative that they collaborate with their colleagues. There are specific employee behaviors which sabotage the production of effective and efficient results and undermine the development of useful working relationships.

The first ineffective way of doing business is aggression. Aggression, or the "fight response," is the kind of behavior which may involve screaming, shouting, pounding a desk and yelling. Here, the employee would use statements which typically begin with the pronoun "you": "You did this to me," "You are miserable to work with," "You are a lousy team player," "You should not be working with me," "You have no right to do that to me," "You are the cause of all my misery," "You are the cause of my failure," "You are going to stop me from being successful."

If these sorts of statements were being hurled at you, you might either run away from the situation or say to yourself, "If this person is going to be aggressive, then I'm going to be aggressive, too." That's why aggression usually achieves very little. People either retreat from you out of fear, or stand their ground and become equally, if not more, aggressive. And so nothing is accomplished. Tension is introduced into the workplace. No positive contribution is made toward the achievement of corporate goals. Your personal objectives are in no way advanced. And, in the long term, your health is likely to suffer.

Type As, mind you, specialize in aggression. They attack their work. They create hostile relationships with their colleagues. They are belligerent with management. It is their misguided belief that if they do not approach matters aggressively, they will never get any work done and will never be successful. Furthermore, they believe that they can exert greater control over their workplace through "a strong offense." They can grab hold of everything and everyone and "shake them into line." Once they dominate their working environment, they can forge ahead to greater heights.

Don't encourage this type of behavior. It breeds resentment, disunity and greater hostility. It does not produce the type of working environment that is conducive to productivity.

Another action which is unsatisfactory and ineffective is avoidance —the "flight response." Here the individual leaves a meeting because she is too anxious or jumpy. Or she dodges a debate with her manager or colleague. When certain Type As become too flustered, frustrated or irritable, when they feel as if they are being challenged or threatened, they make themselves scarce.

Being evasive has some short-term gains. For a brief period of time, you elude the troublesome situation. But over the long term, it is totally useless as a way of managing your affairs. Eventually you need to face up to the situation. But some employees become experts at "dodging bullets." They avoid a wide variety of situations. The sad part of avoidance is that it feels so good—temporarily—that the temptation to repeat it becomes increasingly strong. Sometimes avoidance becomes so much a habit that the individual evades everything that is bothersome. It can become a phobia.

People who are phobic begin to think and believe that they are incapable of facing anything that is troubling to them. Certain Type As can, in the course of time, develop this kind of pattern. They convince themselves that avoidance is not only the easiest, but also the only way out.

But the question remains: how long can anyone keep running away?

Another ineffective pattern is passivity. You remain silent when you are bothered by something. Or you do nothing when a colleague has "dumped" on you. You know very well what you want to say or do, but you don't say it or do it.

Certain Type As at certain times resort to this sort of behavior. They are afraid to upset people. They are apprehensive about asserting their feelings and thoughts to others. If they express themselves openly, they might not receive approval for their actions. Their climb up the ladder of success might be hindered. So they keep their mouths shut until they get so frustrated that they explode in a rage! Then they return to the aggressive mode.

People who become chronically passive suffer a lot of discomfort and agitation. They may be prone to stomach ulcers. Indeed, the passive individual has been referred to as "the ulcerous personality." They allow their internal distress to chew up their stomachs.

Nevertheless, you cannot convince a Type A to sacrifice her passivity. She is absolutely certain that if she remains quiet and never questions anything or anyone she will be regarded as a model employee. She will be seen to be cooperative, pleasant and agreeable and to deserve a better fate.

In some cases, it might be politically wise to keep quiet. But the employee who carries on this way runs the risk of being viewed as a non-contributor, as one who doesn't care or who is afraid to offer an opinion. In the long run, she will have no voice in the decision-making which occurs in her work group. But, more importantly, she will be regarded as having poor communication skills. By adopting a passive strategy, the employee avoids being classed as a troublemaker, but she may still be in trouble.

Type As distort reality and delude themselves. They always believe that their way is the best way. If they are not aggressive, then they may be running away, or they may be running on the spot, doing nothing and remaining passive.

An accountant whom I saw was having problems at work. He explained his predicament this way: "I was always a gung-ho type with my work and with people. Because I approached my job this way, people saw me as aggressive. I guess I did get into more fights than anyone else. But I thought I was doing OK, until one day I received a warning from my manager to stop bullying everyone. I didn't know what to do, because that had always been my style. I got really angry and started to avoid people. If they didn't like who I was, I'd have nothing to do with them. The heck with the team approach! I could do it all by myself. But again, I got another warning, because I wasn't working well with my colleagues. What did they want from me? So you know what I did? I began to go to meetings, but I kept my mouth shut. I would do what they wanted, but I wouldn't say a thing. I figured that this was the best way to get on their good books. There were many times when I wanted to speak up, but I bit my lip instead and kept quiet. But that didn't work either. I was so confused, I gave up!"

The Vicious Stress Cycle

In summary, once you become expert at crooked thinking, it sets the stage for certain uncomfortable feelings and ineffective reactions. If you think that your health and well-being are threatened by occurrences in the workplace which in reality are not so threatening, you will in all likelihood slip into a condition of chronic stress, or a "stress cycle."

This is how it works: We engage in unrealistic thinking which produces feelings of panic, worry or anger, which give rise to inept behavior. As we continue to act ineffectively and fail to produce meaningful results at work, we continue to think even more illogically. As we maintain a course of illogical thinking, we feel even more distress. As we experience even greater distress, we act even more inefficiently. As we persist in our inefficiency, we generate more absurd thoughts. So, round and round it goes, from our thoughts, to our feelings, to our actions, back to our thoughts, and so on. These three reinforce one another, to set up the vicious and pervasive stress cycle.

The Vicious Stress Cycle

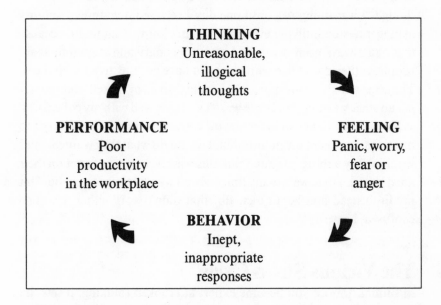

Type As tend to conclude that the cycle will never be broken. They will never achieve anything. They will always be stressed. They will always think that they are going out of their minds. They will always remain on a "stress treadmill," bound for failure, misery and disgrace. Type As get stuck in this cycle because of their inflexibility. They may stay in the same rut indefinitely.

False Strategies

Over the years, we have developed some intriguing coping procedures in an effort to come to grips with stress. These procedures can produce some benefits in the short term, but virtually none in the long term.

These methods are ineffective because they do not alter the thinking process which transforms events in the workplace into potential threats to one's well-being. They are merely palliative, at best.

Many of these activities and strategies may be valuable for their own sake. They may be enjoyable. They may be entertaining as distractions. They become silly and outlandish only when they are used as techniques to eliminate stress.

1: Jogging

Many employees attempt to out-distance their hassles. They suffer from the misguided belief that if they jog, whether at 6:00 A.M. or at midnight, and develop all the aches and pains which are the result of jogging, they will master their stress.

This is grossly inaccurate. As an activity in itself, jogging is valuable. It strengthens the cardiovascular system. It tones muscles. It is useful as an aid in maintaining proper weight. It gives people a high. But as a stress strategy—forget it! I cannot tell you how many people I have encountered who are jogging relentlessly, five or ten miles a day each and every day, who are more fit than you or I will ever be, and yet are complaining of severe stress symptoms. Some admit themselves to emergency wards at their local hospitals, complaining about the fact that they are overwhelmed by anxiety and the related symptoms.

A new problem has now surfaced: compulsive jogging. Some people are driven to jog. If they do not jog, they experience serious anxiety. Missing one or more runs even adds to their stress level. A compulsive jogger not only fails to manage his stress, he heightens it. How many people have you known who, for one reason or another, were not able to jog, and went wild with frustration? They become so anxious, tense and agitated that they are impossible to live with. Obviously, this is not the cure for stress.

2: Aerobics

Aerobic exercise, like jogging, is widely regarded as a panacea for stress. It has gained popularity partly because it is reputed to flush out stress hormones. When a person experiences stress, certain hormones appear in the bloodstream. It has been shown that once an individual exerts herself, these so-called stress hormones all of a sudden disappear from the bloodstream. This has led to the assumption by some people that stress can be controlled through aerobic exercise or other related activities. But if you extend this line of reasoning logically, you would have to exercise perpetually in order to ensure that those stress hormones remain out of the bloodstream. If you do not continue to exercise, the stress hormones might return. And they will return, but because they are linked to your thinking, not because you have stopped exercising.

Aerobic exercise is worthwhile as a short-term measure. Like jogging, it distracts you from your difficulties. It is great for toning and building muscles. It has been described as an aid to reducing blood pressure, to lowering fat and sugar in the bloodstream. These are worthwhile physical results. I believe in exercise. I even have a rowing machine which I use three times a week, for twenty minutes, to ensure that I reach my target heart rate. Exercise is valuable in and of itself, but not as an activity to reduce stress.

3: Tennis and Squash

Colleagues of mine are scrambling all over the tennis and squash courts, convinced that they can beat their stress into submission. But, like other forms of exercise, tennis and squash have absolutely no effect on stress. They may be fun, and good exercise, but as a meaningful, long-term stress-management strategy, they have no merit.

Some people who really get into tennis or squash approach the game the way they approach everything in their lives: they set out to beat their opposition to the ground. If they do not win, they end up more stressed. If you go out of your way to approach these activities aggressively, you can actually bring more stress into your life. You will be stressed going onto the court and coming off the court. You will never get away from stress.

4: Diets

A number of people today are looking for the right diet to manage stress. They believe that if they eat the correct food and provide their bodies with the appropriate nutrients, then they will surely lead a stress-free existence. So they try Scarsdale, or Pritikin, or whatever. They overdose on cottage cheese and fruit. They overdose on pasta, or protein, or carbohydrates. They try starvation. Employees everywhere are seeking more novel, more controversial diets in an effort to change their lives. The most popular lunchtime conversation in many organizations is the diets people are on.

Diets are often seen as magical cures. But we know that after a diet is over, the weight that people have taken off is usually put back on. In fact, people often gain back *more* than they have lost. Consequently, before starting a diet, people are stressed. While on a diet, they are stressed because they are worried about taking off weight. And after the diet is over, when they put weight on again, they are even more stressed!

I would be the last to suggest that food and proper nutrition are not important. Eating a proper balance of the various food groups is essential for daily living. However, food is virtually irrelevant to stress because it does nothing to alter your thinking.

5: *Vitamins*

We are in the midst of a vitamin craze. A vast selection of vitamins is available to help you improve your physical health. "Stress tablets" are among the most popular items in the vitamin market today. People pop these pills as if they are the answer to all woes—then they find that they are still experiencing stress. Vitamins may be valuable, especially to people suffering from a vitamin deficiency. And even people without vitamin deficiencies take vitamins as a supplement to their regular diet. That's fine. But again, vitamins do nothing to change our thinking, and therefore they can do nothing to alleviate the stress which results from our illogical and unreasonable thoughts.

6: *Vacations*

Many people misguidedly believe that they can fly away from their stress.

I recall counseling an airline executive who felt that she had to get away because she was suffering from symptoms of stress. She booked a flight to one of the Caribbean islands, believing that all of her problems would disappear once she was able to take in some sunshine. Once she arrived, she rushed into the hotel and up to her room, tore off her clothes, put on her bathing suit, ran to the beach, threw down a blanket and jumped on the blanket thinking that her problems were gone forever. Two hours later, she was going crazy because she could not get away from the thoughts racing through her mind. She was worrying about what was going on at the office. She was worrying about what was happening at home. She was worrying about all of the work she would have to do when she returned. Two days later she booked a flight home, stressed out of her mind. The vacation had made matters worse.

A lot of people do get more stressed when they are on vacation. I have known a few who have even had heart attacks while on holiday! Of course, a vacation can be restful. But it won't be restful if you expect it to do something it cannot do—that is, eliminate your problems!

It is true that some people are able to work out some of their difficulties while on vacation. They take the time to think and rethink their problems and to formulate some concrete plans to solve them. But not everyone can do this. Some people force holidays on themselves with the underlying condition that they must relax and eliminate their stress. For these individuals, vacations may have the opposite effect.

A restaurant owner came to see me with an interesting dilemma. He admitted that he was a happy workaholic who enjoyed the hustle and bustle of his restaurant business so much that he hadn't taken a vacation in ten years. But his close friends and relatives kept telling him that he was crazy and that everyone needed a holiday. They repeatedly warned him that sooner or later he would crack up. He started to worry that there might be something wrong with him. But this man was simply not interested in a vacation. He enjoyed excellent health. He hadn't been sick a day in his life. Although he didn't see his family as often as he sometimes would have liked to, when they were together they had a wonderful time. They enjoyed walking and talking together, eating together and shopping together. In essence, this man enjoyed life as much as he enjoyed work. He was a contented workaholic who didn't value vacations. I congratulated him for living his life to the fullest.

7: *Hobbies*

I know a number of individuals who have decided to eliminate their stress by taking up hobbies. A route salesperson whom I counseled was particularly disturbed about a rec room he was building. He had bought the best hammer, the right nails and top quality paneling and had set out to hammer away his stress. He would come home from a day on the road frenzied because of the hectic pace, gulp down his dinner and run to the basement to start working on his rec room. He would then labor feverishly until midnight. He was as uptight as could be because things kept going wrong and the room was not going perfectly or fast enough.

This is very common behavior among Type As. They approach everything, including their hobbies, in the same way. They have to do them perfectly. They have to build a better rec room than their neighbor and complete it as quickly as possible. So this particular hobby can stir up considerable agitation, rather than remove it.

Other people try gardening, fishing, motorcycling, playing bridge or simply reading. But a hobby, no matter how interesting, will not lower your stress level. It may be a wonderful diversion, but nothing more. I have been told by hobby enthusiasts: "I know that I relax when I am doing my hobby." And that's great. But when the time for hobbies is over, the hobbyist has to face her problematic situation again. Take up whatever hobby you wish, but bear in mind that it was not intended for the eradication of worries!

8: Sleep

We have all been told to get the proper amount of sleep, so that our bodies will be rested enough to endure the many daily hardships which we encounter. For many, sleep has become a security blanket. But again, sleep has virtually nothing to do with stress.

We know that each of us requires a certain amount of sleep in order to function effectively. We know that different people require different amounts of sleep. We also know that trying to force ourselves to rest more than we really need to can in itself create stress. It may be that some people suffer from sleepless nights because they worry about not getting enough rest! The best advice in such cases is simply to get the rest you need. Beyond that, enjoy the waking hours.

For a few people, slumber can be so wonderful that they would love to sleep away their lives. When they're asleep, they never have to face their problems. But those who become addicted to sleep still have to deal with their troubling situation when they wake.

9: Tranquilizers

Tranquilizers come in all colors and sizes. They are probably as common today as aspirin. They provide a false sense of hope and security. When people take these tablets, they swallow drugs which simply mask the symptoms of stress. When the effects of the tranquilizers wear off, they are once again faced with their problems.

On occasion, people might really require tranquilizers, for a limited time. They are certainly valuable for severe and acute disorders which require temporary medication. So although they may be useful in the short term, in the long term they can be harmful. They can be addictive. And while the symptoms of stress can be severe, trying to withdraw from an addiction to tranquilizers can be a lot worse.

Nevertheless, some people become convinced of tranquilizers' usefulness. They may even trade pills with their colleagues or their next-door neighbors, thinking they are being helpful. But pills do absolutely nothing for your thinking except make it fuzzy.

10: Alcohol

We have all heard about the ravages of chronic alcohol abuse. After a rough day at work, it is not uncommon for groups of workers—or supervisors—to go down to the local pub and "knock back a few drafts." It can easily become a habit. And the habit can easily become an addiction to alcohol. If you think stress is bad, try coming off an addiction to booze.

These are some of the popular coping tools which people commonly use and abuse. I have tried to point out that these strategies do not have any long-term merit, although they may have some short-term benefit. More important, they do not alleviate your stress.

There are some strategies for dealing with stress that *do* work. These strategies are reliable and workable and produce meaningful results. They are not coping tools, but more profound stress-management procedures.

Stress Management by Counterthinking

Relaxation: A Useful First Step

Relaxation can be extremely useful. During times of agitation or heightened arousal, I often practice self-hypnosis. It allows me to reduce the level of uneasiness which I may be experiencing. Once it is diminished, I can carry on more comfortably and effectively. However, beyond this very important short-term benefit, I have difficulty seeing this technique as a major strategy for eliminating stress.

There are those who would have us believe that the ideal state is one of relaxation. If a stressed individual learns to relax, this argument goes, then she will be able to develop a stress-free existence. This is utter nonsense! No one can remain tranquil for twenty-four hours a day. No one can perform efficiently on the job while remaining completely at rest. We all require a certain level of arousal and excitement—of positive stress—in order to be effective. Only when the arousal level becomes too great is it worthwhile to use a relaxation method.

I recall an athlete whom I counseled. In our discussions we talked about the merits of relaxation as well as its limitations. It was obviously important to learn how to relax but it was useful to apply the technique discriminately. If he was too uptight or too nervous, he would practice it. But relaxation was not a state he sought before a big game. He enjoyed being energized and psyched up for the competition. He found that being invigorated, fired up and stimulated helped his performance tremendously. One time, he tried relaxing before a game. He certainly felt tranquil and at peace with himself, but his performance was less than adequate.

Some people get even more stressed by trying too hard to relax. They demand instant results. They believe that they should be able to relax with the same efficiency that they display in performing other tasks. So, in typical Type A fashion, they get even more uptight.

We have been inventive over the years, discovering a lot of weird and wonderful ways to relax ourselves.

The fad one year was "pyramid power." Busy employees, after a hard day's work, would come home, toss their briefcases aside, perhaps tear their clothes off, and place themselves under a pyramid. The idea was that after a period of time, they would step out and be totally and completely at peace with themselves. Now this fad faded into oblivion, as most fads do. But while it lasted, some people were able to brag to their colleagues that they had been helped by this wonderful structure which they believed—and the key word here is "believed"—had had a mystical effect on them. Who knows? Maybe it did.

Then someone discovered the "charged particles" that were moving in the air. They become concerned that an ion imbalance—too many positive ions and too few negative ions—was causing employees to become uptight. They thought that if the correct concentration of negative ions was pumped into the air, employees would be more relaxed and do their jobs more effectively. Many companies purchased their own ion machines. Nothing happened. People were no more relaxed, nor did they perform any better, although they certainly had a different concentration of ions in their environments.

Certain sports teams who were doing poorly tried ionization. As you may have guessed, after they bombarded themselves with negative ions, they continued to play poorly.

A recent phenomenon is a tank used to induce sensory deprivation. If you saw the movie *Altered States*, you will know what I am talking about. In the movie, the star researcher placed himself in a tank that was filled with salt water. Once in this tank, he was deprived of stimulation.

He could hear nothing, see nothing, smell nothing. He was simply suspended in water. He could only go with his thoughts and feelings. After a period of time, he drifted into a comfortable state of rest and peacefulness, which is rightly referred to as an altered state of consciousness. The problem is that if anyone is deprived of all sensory stimulation for too long a time, that person begins to hallucinate. This happened to the researcher in the movie, and the story carried on.

Some clever marketing experts have now made these tanks available to the public. Picture a harassed, stressed employee who comes home and wants to relax. He strips and enters this tank filled with salt water. He closes the door behind him. He floats in the water for a while, then comes out looking like a prune. Is he any more relaxed? Maybe he is, for a little while. But he has also made himself look ridiculous. No one needs such an elaborate contraption just to get a little peace. If you want some quiet time to yourself, you can find it in the privacy of your office. If your office isn't private, you might consider going to the washroom for a short time. It certainly isn't any more ridiculous than a tank.

When you find a quiet place, close the door, switch off the lights and hold all telephone calls. Seat yourself in a comfortable chair and close your eyes. Now you have almost all the advantages of a tank, with the added advantages of convenience and practicality!

If you are not keen on any of these fads, it might be worth your while to consider some more practical techniques to induce relaxation. These procedures include yoga, meditation, biofeedback, autogenic training, progressive muscle relaxation and hypnosis. The emphasis in these cases is not on gadgetry. Instead, you learn to control the level of arousal in your body, so that ultimately you are able to bring on a restful, peaceful state, which is an "altered state" of consciousness. One procedure is not necessarily better than the others; each tends to produce a similar state of relaxation. There have been many books and articles written about these techniques. Find a book on one that interests you, take a course from a reputable instructor, and discover for yourself what it is all about.

It is critical that you work with a qualified practitioner, one who is knowledgeable and experienced in the particular technique you wish to use and whose credentials are clearly established. There are many people who claim to be able to teach one or more of these techniques, but are not properly qualified. Too often people spend more time shopping for the right deodorant than for assistance that will improve their health. So take this particular shopping escapade very seriously and spend some time checking out what is best for you.

When you learn a relaxation procedure and become skilled in its use, you will have achieved a considerable goal. Ideally, you should be able to use your procedure in the office, or in a meeting, or in any given situation that is important to you. It will take continued practice, but it will be well worth the effort.

I was working with an individual who was extremely agitated, discouraged and nervous in a variety of situations. He was jumpy in meetings. He was tense when he met people and when he had to go into his supervisor's office. It was important for him to reduce his level of arousal in these circumstances, because these activities were an important part of his working day. So I taught him to hypnotize himself.

When he started the program it took him approximately half an hour to bring about a reasonable state of relaxation. However, he worked at the technique diligently and persistently. With continued practice, he was able to reduce the amount of time he needed to relax himself to approximately ten seconds. Once he became adept, he began to find that he could employ this method in meetings, in the office with his manager or supervisor, and in various encounters with his colleagues. In essence, he was able to relax himself without the people around him noticing. He was thoroughly delighted with his results.

This example is not necessarily the goal to be aimed for immediately. (No doubt Type As would strive for five seconds, or even less, as long as they had the lowest figure on record.) It is, however, important to practice frequently so that you can relax yourself quickly enough to deal on the spot with troubling situations at work, without the technique being conspicuous or apparent to anyone.

Time Management: An Obvious Procedure

Most of us have heard about, read about, or even been exposed to time management procedures. Time management underlines the importance of planning and emphasizes the usefulness of setting priorities. In essence, people are urged to keep a log of the tasks which require completion and to order them so that the most urgent and critical jobs are finished first. This seems to make sense, because it forces you to examine what you do and how you do it, in order to avoid being overwhelmed by the many jobs which you may be expected to accomplish. Time management has, in turn, been regarded as a major stress-management tool, because of its emphasis on time control and the regulation of work.

Time-management experts have, among other things, told us how to manage our phone calls effectively. They suggest arranging calls in various piles according to their importance. The first pile would be essential calls which require an immediate response. The remaining piles, in order of importance, could be addressed when you have sufficient time. You simply prioritize your phone calls just as you prioritized your tasks.

You may also keep an account of your activities aside from phone calls and other tasks. You can determine how much time you spend on each activity, and decide whether you are making judicious use of each hour during the working day. If you spend too many hours on activities which do not help you to meet your goals, you should put these aside in favor of activities that contribute to your objectives.

Time-management procedures have also been applied to activities outside the work environment. It has been pointed out that if you govern your time carefully, you will have greater opportunities to enjoy your family and friends; you will have the chance to engage in various forms of exercise; you will be able to indulge in recreational activities or simply relax. Basically time management gives you the opportunity to enjoy an enriched and balanced life.

By paying close attention to how you spend your time, and eliminating wastage, your quality of life both on and off the job should be greatly enhanced. It follows that stress will also be minimized.

However, as with any technique, there is a tendency among many employees to adopt it temporarily and then disregard it. It is almost like trying to lose weight. We are really keen at the beginning, and we may drop five or ten pounds. But after a while we are not so eager any more, and we put on the original five or ten pounds, and maybe gain a few extra. The same reaction takes place with time-management procedures. We try them for a while, and everything seems to be working out. Then we drift back to our old ways of doing things.

The procedures are well founded. They make a lot of sense. But they also require some mental discipline. When I talk about "mental," I mean thinking. If we start haphazardly to do something without thinking about what we are doing or why we are doing it, we will eventually stop doing it, and that in itself can trigger stress.

As I mentioned earlier, we are all in the habit of running around and doing, doing, doing. Eventually, we tend to forget why we are doing what we are doing, or whether it is even worthwhile. A good example of this is meetings. We all know that there is value in meeting with colleagues and management to arrive at a solution to a particular problem or to come to a decision about an important query. It may be necessary to have a meeting because a number of key people will be influenced by the decision and it would be wise to gauge their reactions. It may also be essential to hold a meeting because the input of influential individuals is required in order to arrive at a meaningful solution. But it is all too easy to get caught up in meetings. It is not unusual to find that after one meeting, an additional meeting is organized. And then you have a third meeting about the second meeting which was about the first meeting.

Eventually you have to throw up your hands and ask yourself, "Why am I doing this?"

Similarly, it is possible to get so buried in time-management techniques that we become obsessed with arranging our schedules, coordinating our activities, streamlining our timetables and basically overmanaging our lives. Then we get so fed up that we drop the whole thing and go back to old ways of doing business. But discarding everything makes no sense either. Time-management principles are valuable if we are prepared to use them reasonably. Think before you do!

An insurance broker described her dilemma to me: "I've always been too busy. The first week that I got into insurance, I was already up to my ears in potential business. I've been successful over the years, but I have often wondered whether I could be more successful. Maybe if I was better organized, I could write up even more business. So some colleagues and I took a course on how to manage time more effectively. It was great. Everybody raved about it. But I didn't get the results I wanted. Maybe it wasn't for me, or maybe I simply wasn't using it properly. Everything was supposed to be monitored—my phone calls, my meetings, my discussions with people, my 'cold calls,' my meal breaks. I spent so much time keeping track of everything that it cut into my selling time. Then I began to ask myself why I was doing this. It's really not like me to be so picky and precise and plan every detail of my life. I got so frustrated that I dropped the whole thing! This move ended up being the right one for me."

It is important both on an individual level and on a corporate scale to value the reflective and introspective process as much as, if not more than, the action process. Whether it has to do with time-management practices, new methods of entrepreneurship (or "intrapreneurship," which is entrepreneurship inside the organization), new management techniques, or methods of improved communication, it is still important to step back and examine motives. Contemplation will often clarify the purposes, goals and reasons for following through on a particular enterprise. If you think before you act, you are likely to act much more effectively. If you reflect before you implement time-management procedures, you are likely not only to benefit by their use, but also to use them over a longer period of time. But if after thinking about them you decide not to use these procedures, you will be able to discard them knowing you have made a reasonable and considered decision.

Counterthinking

We discussed earlier the damaging effects of "stinking thinking," or thinking which produces stress. If thinking is critical in producing stress, it is also critical in managing stress. Earlier I discussed thinking which is unrealistic, irrational, unreasonable and ultimately unproductive. This thinking can be changed to become rational, reasonable and productive.

You are in control of how you reason! If you have created your own silly thinking, then you can "uncreate" it and create something else in its place. If you created thinking which produced stress, then you can create more realistic thinking to minimize your stress.

In an earlier section, I described a number of typical thoughts "guaranteed to drive you nuts." Now I propose to take these nutty ideas and create more reasonable ones. This is the essence of counterthinking. If you adopt this approach, you will find it much easier to manage your work. You will find that you feel better. You will discover that you are more productive. You will notice that you get along much better with your colleagues and management. You will perceive a greater sense of well-being. Most important, you will manage your stress!

1. Mistakes happen and nothing terrible results.
If a mistake is made, the world will certainly not come to an end. For some perfectionists, this is quite an eye-opener; others simply refuse to accept it. But we all stumbled before we learned to walk. We all stuttered before we learned to put a proper sentence together. And we have learned from our mistakes.

If we can accept the fact that we learn from our mistakes, then we can acknowledge that it is not so terrible to make them. But there are many Type As who believe that you must get things right the first time, or forget it.

Don't forget it; learn from it.

An aside: I think that one of the most important things which we can do as parents is to teach our children how to fail. If we allow our children to explore their environment, make mistakes and fall flat on their faces, and in the process point out that it is not terrible to fail, that this is how people learn, these children will not fear failure or crave perfection as adults. Too often we demand too much. We demand perfection when it comes to schoolwork. We demand that they get things right. If we took the approach that we can all learn from our blunders, then children could handle their so-called failures more easily and excel.

In the workplace, there is the same intolerance for mistakes. No employee ever receives a pat on the back for making a blunder. It's rare that an employee receives a kind word for learning from a failure.

But we know that nothing awful will result if we do make an error. There may be some heat directed our way, but that typically subsides, especially if we make the necessary corrections the next time. Only if we continually and regularly repeat the same errors are we likely to run into serious trouble.

2. *There is clearly no right and wrong way to do things.*
What is right for one situation or person may not be right for another. There is a lot of gray between black and white. We all know that in the world of business there are few rules carved in stone. If we accept this and work with it, it makes life in the workplace quite a bit easier.

Some employers might argue the point. They might claim that the bottom line is always right, and that the bottom line is that you must make a profit, no matter what! But it's not so simple. Making a profit unethically, for example, or to the detriment of the customer or the client, is not necessarily right. Sometimes short-term gain may lead to long-term loss. So once again, it is important to examine our thinking. We have to use our best judgment. We have to do the best we can, in an exciting environment which, I believe, is built on a foundation of risk-taking and entrepreneurship, and not on a groundwork of right and wrong.

3. I will accept criticism and see how I can benefit from it.

This also means that I will keep my mind open to feedback. If the criticism is constructive and it makes sense to me, I will take it seriously enough to attempt to act on it. On the other hand, if the criticism is destructive and does not make sense to me, then I will accept the fact that my critic is entitled to his or her opinion. This thinking, surely, is quite a bit more reasonable and more realistic than fearful thinking. Criticism does not necessarily have to be equated with failure.

If we could also teach our children to accept criticism, in the same way we teach them to accept mistakes, they might be a lot healthier and happier. Certainly these children, as eventual adults in the workplace, would perform and produce far more effectively.

4. I will not demand approval.

No one needs approval in order to do his or her best, although it is certainly nice to receive it. There is no rule or regulation which stipulates that you have to have approval in order to do your job. You do not have to receive "positive strokes" each and every day in order to be productive. If we needed approval in order to produce, then no one would be producing in the workplace. Certain employees see approval as being almost like food and drink. They think that they need it in order to survive.

Some management training experts might disagree. They would indicate that it is important to offer positive feedback and approval, especially when work is well done. I have no quarrel with this. As a psychologist, I understand the merits of positive reinforcement. If one completes a project successfully, it is certainly nice to receive support and approval. However, there is a difference between appreciating approval and demanding that you receive it from everyone around you. Employees who demand it but don't receive it are in deep trouble. They end up stressing themselves needlessly. They also draw all sorts of negative conclusions about how poorly they must be doing, because they did not receive their quota of positive strokes. This ends up hurting their productivity.

Many individuals in the workplace find it difficult to give positive feedback. Do not jump to conclusions about your performance if you do not receive the approval which you believe is your due. When you do receive endorsement, enjoy it. But there is no assurance that you will continue to receive approval, and it is important not to demand it.

5. I will not demand that I be competent, but I will certainly strive for it.
There are many employees who seriously and earnestly believe that they must be unfailingly competent at everything they attempt; otherwise, they are outright failures. Type As are notorious for this. But hardly anyone is competent at everything. It doesn't follow that we are all failures. It simply means that we are more capable at some activities than at others.

We can certainly strive to be skilled at everything we try, but if it doesn't work out, the world won't end. But some people carry the thought around in their heads that total and complete competence is critical. They set themselves up for some uncomfortable discoveries.

A complementary thought: I will accept the fact that people will not always see me the way I would like to be seen. If a person can't always be competent, it follows that management may not always rate him highly, and his colleagues may not always view him as being totally capable.

Again, it is one thing to accept that we are fallible, and quite another to believe that we have failed miserably. In fact, the way in which we are judged is quite complicated. Work performance and competence are not the sole determinants of how we are rated. There are other subtle elements, such as social skills, "people" skills, and other intangibles, which enter into any rating of one person by another. The rating is often more subjective than objective. So why get hung up on it?

You have no control over how others view you. It is in the hands of the person who is carrying out the rating, whether it be management or colleagues or friends. The priority for you, as an employee, is to simply do your best each and every day. Then, more often than not, things will work out the way you wish them to. And isn't that pretty good? You might wish to be rated as perfect. But perfection is an illusion. And since we are talking about realistic and reasonable thinking in this case, then please discard your illusions.

6. *I will not be fearful in the presence of authority.*
You *can* challenge what people say and do, in a constructive fashion, and nothing catastrophic will happen. This is a major problem for certain employees, especially administrative employees who perform clerical functions. Clerical people are among the most stressed groups of employees. All sorts of ideas run through their minds, many of which are unrealistic and unreasonable. They believe that their supervisors and managers are like gods. They are afraid to challenge them. And yet they go around complaining, griping and cursing the day they came into the workplace. They complain not to the people who are important, but to their colleagues. If their thinking was more rational, they would approach their managers and supervisors and talk things through.

You can approach people in authority and work out your disagreements. You can present your ideas in a constructive fashion. Doom will rarely result. This is not to say that you have a written guarantee that everything will turn out just the way you want it to. But in most cases, most of the time, things will probably work out. You are not likely to be fired or demoted. And you may discover that the person in authority appreciates your input.

Of course, communication in the workplace has always been important. Many of us know this, but we still experience communication breakdowns. We still foul up. We assume that because we are knowledgable in communication skills, strategies and techniques, we will obtain what we want from those we work with. We assume that if only we express ourselves openly and let our feelings be known, our colleagues and managers will take note. When the results which we expect are not forthcoming, we throw up our hands in frustration, anger and indignation and say, "The heck with this."

Clerical and administrative staff are notorious for this. When they have got up the nerve to talk to their superiors, and their superiors have not given them what they wanted, they withdraw, muttering furiously that they will never communicate what they feel again. Such people give up too easily. They demand results from just one exchange. But dialogue is ongoing. Communication is never-ending. The channels for talking and negotiating should always be open. This, then, is another example of thinking which leads inevitably to frustration.

7. I accept the fact that life in the workplace is not always fair and just.
This means that neither your colleagues nor your managers have to agree with what you say. For many employees, this is very, very difficult to accept. But let's face it: things are not always equitable and impartial. And if they were, it would not necessarily imply that the people you work with had to pay attention to you. This is reality!

You can argue that you're not going to stand for it. You can swear that you're going to make it better, more fair, more just. But you can't, can you? Maybe a few individuals have the power to create an environment just the way they envision it. But most of us mere mortals do not. If you demand this power, you are putting yourself in an awkward and stressful position.

In fact, a workplace that does *not* respond instantly to one person's idea of what is just is more likely to be productive than one that does. There are benefits to disagreement. Often some of the best solutions result from controversy. Those who insist that their workplace be calm and settled, and that everyone concur with them, have unrealistic expectations. Constructive controversy can be meaningful and productive.

8. I give myself the right to be out of control once in a while.
This means that you will not always be alert or brilliant. After all, who do you know who is always alert and brilliant? Even presidents and prime ministers have their bad days. Yet there are employees who persist in demanding perfect control from themselves. They pigheadedly believe that only if they are flawless in their conduct will they be successful, productive and stress-free.

There is no question that people like to take charge of their lives. Employees appreciate knowing what they need to do in order to excel at their jobs. But to believe that they have to perform in a dazzling manner in order to get ahead is stretching it. They can only strive to do their best. If their performance is not splendid, then at least they did their best. That, surely, is something to take pride in.

The issue of control seems to be central in any discussion of stress. Some people have been led to believe that if they are in control of their lives, they will experience no stress. On the surface, this seems to make a lot of sense. But what happens when, for whatever reason, they are not able to rule their activities in the way they believe they should? Say, for example, that an employee has not met a target date for the completion of a particular project. Or, simply, an employee ends up feeling bored on the job. What are they to do? Well, many Type As go to pieces. They start to think in terms of doom and gloom. They start to believe that their productivity will deteriorate until they hit rock bottom.

If you tend to think along these lines, why don't you make work easier for yourself? It is very appealing to think that you can take charge of your working life, but you can't always. If you permit yourself the luxury of being tolerant of your own occasional, unintentional errors, it takes the pressure off. Now you might say, "I won't be as productive," or "I won't be as successful." In fact, you will be even more successful and more productive, and achieve your goals more often, because, instead of focusing on being in control all the time, you will be focusing on what you want out of life. That means directing your attention to your objectives and what you wish to achieve.

9. *I can neither anticipate nor be certain of everything.*

Many Type As seem to think that it is necessary to be a step ahead of everybody. They have to know what is going on not only in the minds of their managers, but also in the minds of their colleagues. If they are a step ahead, this will surely guarantee prosperity!

Of course, the difficulty is that it is not always possible to determine what is going on in people's minds. Still, some Type As seem to think that they are so gifted, intuitive or perceptive that they can always second-guess everybody. Many claim, for example, to be able to read people's "vibrations." They believe that they have a sixth sense, by which they are capable of reading non-verbal messages, voice intonations and facial expressions. Clearly, these "readings" are nothing more than guesswork, but certain employees act as if they constituted certain knowledge and actually base decisions on them. Then they are dumbfounded when things don't work out the way they expected them to. It is important to respond to what we see and hear, but even the most perceptive observer can't predict too much for certain. Even our meteorologists have given up trying to forecast the weather accurately. They now talk in terms of the chances of rain, or the probability of snow. Isn't life really one big probability?

10. *I accept the fact that I will not always get what I want, though I will continue to strive for it.*

In other words, if things don't come your way as quickly as possible, namely the good salary, the beautiful office, the prestigious position, you won't be heartbroken for the rest of your life. Type As tend to be immune to such rational thinking. However, acceptance of this more reasonable and realistic thought makes life quite a bit easier. It certainly makes it possible to contain stress symptoms.

There are still many employees who demand everything from life and expect to get it all immediately. Obviously, they are in for a big disappointment. An individual may be fortunate enough to experience a string of successes. But if she goes on to believe that this string will continue for the whole of her career, she has made a major thinking error. The fact that four consecutive items on her "to do" list worked out just the way she planned them does not ensure that Item 5, Item 6 or Item 10 will work out too. Certain employees are not prepared for this reality, and they run into trouble.

I have heard employees say, with complete conviction, that if they are not demanding on the job, they will never get what they want! But try to allow for the fact that things might not always be the way you want them to be.

11. I will give others the right to be wrong, and will not be angry or hostile toward them.

This makes a lot of sense, but to Type As, mistakes are intolerable. They believe that when people make errors, they deserve to be punished. It is not, therefore, surprising that Type As are so angry and hostile toward others.

This attitude does not really make for cooperative relationships in the workplace. The notion of teamwork is very important today in many companies. But how can we expect to get teamwork from a person who is always judging other people? Type As constantly set themselves up as judge and jury to those around them. They are constantly on guard to see who goofs and who does not. Those who slip up, those who are fallible and those who are not absolutely efficient should, in their view, bear the harshest consequences.

If you can accept that you are imperfect, it becomes easier to accept imperfection in others. There are those who say that if you put up with anything less than perfection, you will make errors all the time. You will never be a success. You will fail at your job. But this is neither logical nor realistic. People who try to do their best, to be as productive as they can, will nevertheless have occasional slipups. Why condemn them for it? Why be angry and hostile toward them? It makes life a lot easier for you and your colleagues if you accept your own and other people's mistakes. This principle may sound almost spiritual or religious. I view it as a certain philosophical style that aids in reducing and managing stress. Acceptance, tolerance, patience, allowance for imperfections: these are critical when we talk about controlling stress. And all these terms have to do with your outlook and with your thinking.

12. If I do not receive full support and enjoy a caring attitude from people around me, it will not be the end of the world.
There are employees who, when they are not as productive or as successful as they believe they should be, cry the blues and expect that everybody will be sympathetic to their cause. And if people are not sympathetic, they begin to hate everyone and to loathe their work environment. This kind of reaction is damaging to the individual and to work morale. If things don't go right on the job, for whatever reason, it would be great to get consolation from others, but what if it doesn't happen? Well, some Type As get more miserable and depressed, and finally more stressed. They formulate silly conclusions. For them it is proof positive that the world is mean, rotten, uncaring, unresponsive and miserable. This is complete nonsense.

Colleagues, supervisors, and managers will not always come across the way that you expect. Why not realize that? Why not give up that demand? Why not adopt a more reasonable approach to the whole situation? If things don't work out on the job for one reason or another, and people are not overflowing with condolences, it is unfortunate, but not the end of the world. Maybe tomorrow your colleagues will be more sympathetic to your cause. But you must realize that concern and care are not like food and drink. You do not need them to survive. Leave yourself alone. Leave others alone. If others choose to be considerate (and some of them will), enjoy it. But if they are not, it doesn't really matter.

13. *I accept the fact that I will not feel superb all of the time.*
Certain Type As won't accept this proposition. They demand that they feel great each and every day. By "feeling great" they really mean that they must never get anxious, worried, jumpy, tense or stressed. Is this realistic? Of course not. But when Type As are not feeling just right, they start to panic. They begin to brood. They worry about not feeling well. Then they worry about the fact that they are worrying about not feeling well. Sound mixed up? It is! This is what stress is all about. Why get into this vicious cycle? We are not machines; we are human beings who are capable of experiencing the full range of emotions. This is what makes living and working so exciting: the ups and downs, the challenges, the defeats, the victories, and so on.

If you demand that you only feel up, happy, ecstatic, joyous, exuberant, ebullient, energetic and zestful, isn't your goal going to be rather difficult to achieve? It certainly would be exhausting! So get your thinking in line. Be a little more flexible and pragmatic. Allow for the full range of human experience. With luck, you will feel reasonably well and be reasonably productive most of the time. But if you get hung up on feeling on top of the world all of the time, I can almost assure you that you won't be very productive. You will be too worried about not being 100 percent.

14. *I will not judge myself according to what I do or don't do.*
When an employee's performance is judged, it is *only* the performance that is judged, not the person's worth as an employee. Type As are notorious for thinking that if their performance isn't what it should be, they must be complete misfits and failures. Things are fine when their performance appraisals are good, but all hell breaks loose if they are unsatisfactory. But just because a person receives a mediocre or poor performance appraisal for a certain period does not mean that he should renounce his status as a member of the human race!

When your work is reviewed, you have an opportunity to think about your performance and make the improvements that are necessary. But if you are obsessed with the rating which you receive, you will not pay attention to the corrections that need to be made, but instead focus on how rotten a human being you must be. And if you concentrate on that, you will be stressed and depressed. So leave yourself alone. Management has the right to judge your accomplishments. It is part of their function. Work with the appraisal, but don't draw conclusions about yourself. Draw conclusions about your productivity and try to improve on it.

15. I was not promised a corporate rose garden.

Work is not always rewarding, and colleagues and managers are not always considerate, kind and respectful. Doesn't knowing this make life in the workplace a little easier? Doesn't this take the pressure off you? Now you can roll with the punches. You can be more flexible. When your work happens to be gratifying and stimulating and your colleagues are cooperative and attentive, you can rejoice. When work is not as fulfilling and your colleagues are not so accommodating, then you can tolerate that, too. It will be possible for you to work through mundane projects, handle less satisfying tasks and details, deal with uncompromising colleagues and not get so hung up about it.

16. It is not too late for me to change.

You alone are responsible for your life and career. You are capable of recognizing changes that need to be made in your behavior, and are capable of making those modifications if you wish to.

Why do you think performance appraisals have gained such prominence in the workplace? They provide a major opportunity for the manager or supervisor and the employee to sit down and discuss their problems. Together, they can talk about what has and has not been accomplished. Granted, these sessions are not always objective, but, with luck, they are enlightening most of the time. More important, if the employee is reasonable enough to consider the feedback which she receives, then she can make a calculated decision about what changes she chooses to make. People who always complain, who are cynical and who reject change are the ones who experience stress. Those who let it be known to colleagues and management that they are open-minded and adaptable, and are prepared to consider other ways of doing business, can only be admired by those they work with.

An actuary whom I counseled offered a revealing commentary. "My career and my life in general were always filled with rules and regulations. There was a right and a wrong way to do things. Basically, I thought that living should be an exact science. In other words, if I did something, then I believed that I should get a certain reaction. For example, if I worked very hard to complete a particular project, then my manager should applaud my efforts, reward my accomplishments and sing my praises for a job well done. Boy, was I let down!

"Also, I was a chronic perfectionist and a chronic worrier. What a combination! I was truly unhappy. I was always asking myself if this was the way I wanted to be for the rest of my life. And I always came up with the same answer—no. After all, how many lives did I have?

"Yet there was a choice: I could continue to drive myself into the ground, or I could change. So I dedicated myself to doing things differently. I made a point of not worrying. I made a point of accepting that I wasn't perfect and my work wasn't perfect. I made a point of accepting that not everyone approved of me and of the work I did. I made a point of believing that I could only do my best and, after that, let the chips fall where they may. You know, it made a tremendous difference. It was as if a big load had been removed from my shoulders. What a relief! I feel much better. Now I enjoy life. Also—and this is really funny —my work is better and I get along better with people."

If you can adopt and subscribe to reasonable, rational and realistic thinking, it sets the stage for a profound reduction in your stress symptoms. Remember, if stress originates in the mind, it is there that you have to look first for solutions. If you make these necessary shifts in your thinking, you will find that stress can be contained and controlled, to the point where you can manage your working life effectively and efficiently.

Positive Thinking: Too Much of a Good Thing

You are probably aware of a major psychological trend in business and industry called "positive thinking" or "the power of positive thinking." You may have read books about it. You may even have experimented with it, and found that it did not produce the desired results.

In fact, positive thinking may actually increase stress. This may sound like a major contradiction. You would think that once you start to think positively, stress would be eliminated, because stress has to do with negative thinking. If only you replace the negative with more positive thinking, that should be the answer. That is not always the case, however —in a number of situations, positive thinking makes matters worse.

Positive thinking came into prominence because it was felt that people who performed poorly were cynical, pessimistic, gloomy and dismal. So it was deemed necessary that these people should be taught to think with optimism, inspiration and promise. Then their performance would turn around, and they would once again proceed on the road to success. If employees regularly repeated optimistic statements to themselves, thought very positively and looked to the future with buoyancy and enthusiasm, there would be extraordinary improvement at work, and life would be rosy. This seems logical on the surface, but once you examine the reasoning closely, you can begin to see the cracks and flaws.

Let's take an example. Sally works for a placement agency and is a good employee. She has been doing well on the job over the years. Lately, however, things are not working out. She is stressed. She notices that she is jumpy and irritable, not the calm and efficient person she would like to be. One day she finds out about positive thinking, and she starts to practice it. In the mornings, she wakes up and repeats the following messages to herself: "Today is going to be the best working day ever. Today I am going to meet all my deadlines. Today I am going to get along with everybody. Today I am going to impress my manager. Today is going to be the most fantastic day I have ever experienced. Furthermore, I am going to be in complete control. I am going to feel great. I am going to feel wonderful. I am going to think clearly." After saying all of this, she feels very psyched up.

Many sports teams are big on positive thinking. It is not unusual to find athletes in the locker room before a big game psyching themselves up. They might say to themselves: "I am going to be dynamite. I am going to perform fantastically. I am going to destroy my opposition. I am going to play the greatest game I ever played in my life. I am going to tear them apart. I am going to show more energy than I ever displayed in my life. I am going to be extraordinary. I am going to be mean. I am going to win." After they repeat these expressions, they run onto the field, or onto the court, or onto the ice, and expect miraculous things to happen. They assume that once they have said positive things to themselves, then they are bound to perform positively.

But there is a problem. Once our employee has recited all of those encouraging expressions to herself, what happens when she comes to work and events don't develop the way she thought they would? How will she react? How is she going to feel? You might suggest that if things don't work out, it's because she didn't think positively enough. But that is not true. It happens, sometimes, that employees do think positively, but the world doesn't cooperate. Circumstances in the workplace do not fall into place. Sally may be unnecessarily causing herself a lot of grief by truly believing that just because her outlook is extremely optimistic, everything will work out positively. Can we really predict how things are going to work out? Can we really forecast how we are going to get along with people? Can we really determine how management is going to react to us? Can we really foresee with certainty that all of the project deadlines will be met? No!

So do not place yourself in this particular bind. Even soothsayers cannot predict everything, especially everything positive, that will occur. With luck, good fortune will come your way, and you will be rewarded for your efforts, but there is no guarantee. Of course, this isn't good enough for the Type A personality. Type As are especially prone to adopt positive thinking. And when positive things don't materialize, they ruin themselves psychologically. They experience more stress than ever before. They used this positive thinking, which they believed was so powerful, and it didn't even work! They take this to be unequivocal proof that they will be stressed for the rest of their lives, they will never succeed, they will never amount to anything, and they will be doomed for eternity.

Positive thinking has some merit, because it heightens your arousal. It does psych you up; it does mobilize your energies and get you prepared for the working day. But it does not guarantee positive results. Nor does it necessarily eliminate stress. What I am suggesting, therefore, is that you recognize the limits of the procedure and use it with some caution.

Talking to Yourself Is OK

Remember how people used to say that if you talked to yourself you were a little bit nutty, but if you answered yourself you were really nutty? Things have changed. Now we have legitimized internal dialogue, or "self-talk." Since we are prone to unhealthy thinking and because we now understand that unsound logic contributes to our stress, it's OK to talk to ourselves and challenge what is going on in our minds. How do we do this? Let me offer you some questions which you can pose to yourself. These queries will make it possible for you to confront your illogic, to counter your faulty reasoning, to call into question your poor judgment. This process should assist you to change your thinking, so that you come up with a more reasonable and realistic perspective.

The next time you experience stress, ask yourself the following questions:

What thought just went through my head?

Does that thought actually make sense?

Is there any evidence to support that thought?

How do I know that thought to be true?

If you consider these questions carefully, you will quickly realize that there is not much evidence for your particular thought. The idea does not make much sense. It is not realistic. Knowing this, you can begin to replace your illogical thought with a more sensible and rational one.

Can you begin to see what is happening? You are becoming your own counselor. You are beginning to challenge your thinking as it has never been challenged before. You are overturning the reasoning that caused your stress. In doing this, you should be inspired to generate more credible and well-founded thoughts, to replace the unreasonable ideas which have plagued you for so long.

When you are stressed you can also ask yourself the following question: *"What is the worst thing that can happen to me?"* In answering this question, you will begin to appreciate that nothing too terrible is likely to happen. No catastrophe will occur. Your life will not be threatened. Your well-being will not be jeopardized. Your career will not be totally and completely damaged. Once you develop this healthier perspective, it will have a tremendous impact on your stress level.

The superintendent of a school board once offered these words of wisdom to me: "Do you know how I manage stress? I argue with myself. I debate with myself. I examine my logic to determine its sense, suitability and rationality. You see, I have a very active mind, which sometimes gets me into real trouble. But I also have the capability to change what goes on in my head. Often my colleagues find me walking down the halls mumbling to myself. But it works. First I talk to myself and come up with a more reasonable outlook on the particular matter at hand. Then I decide whether I need to do anything different. In a way, I've become my own therapist, and I don't even have a Ph.D. in psychology!"

Another question that you can ask yourself is this: *"Where is it written that I have to do this or that, or that life has to be this way, or that some person should act that way?"* In responding to this query, you will soon recognize that there are no rules "carved in stone." You don't have to do this or that. People do not have to behave toward you in a certain way. Work does not have to offer the ultimate in perfection and reward. Again, you can begin to appreciate that this self-talk is very worthwhile, because it is loaded with common sense, solid logic and profound realism. And again, you can see that if you get involved in this question-and-answer thinking, it will have a favorable impact on your stress.

So try to become an expert at talking to yourself. Ask yourself questions which probe, investigate and explore the ideas that you believe in, that comprise your philosophy and that have brought you stress and grief. Having posed the questions, try to come up with reasonable answers. When you have worked out your answers, adopt them as your new philosophy, as your new way of looking at the world. Embrace them as your new way of viewing the workplace. Once you have been able to do this, and have made a habit of doing it, you will start to sense that stress is manageable and is under your control.

Using Your Imagination

We all have imaginations. Some of us use them in weird and wonderful ways. Type As often use them to create stress rather than to relieve it.

People who are stressed, particularly Type As, often develop powerful pictures in their minds of doom and gloom. They contrive images that are traumatic. They fabricate imaginary catastrophes. Their minds seem to spawn scenes which contribute to their anxiety. Let me give you an example.

A situation which provokes a great deal of stress for many employees is public speaking. Many people dread making presentations to their colleagues and managers. Being skilled at public speaking has a pretty good payoff: if you are capable of making good presentations, you are likely to receive praise and positive performance appraisals, and you might even be considered for a promotion somewhat earlier than expected. But employees who are disturbed about the prospect of making a presentation usually have frantic imaginations. They visualize a scene which is bound to upset them and may ultimately hurt their chances of delivering a satisfactory talk.

They might, for example, picture themselves as somewhat jumpy a couple of days prior to the talk. They see themselves finding it difficult to sleep well, eat regularly and socialize with others, particularly with people at work. They visualize themselves working very hard at the presentation, yet not feeling assured. On the morning of the presentation, they picture themselves feeling very upset. They may be nauseated, unable to eat breakfast, unable to get dressed properly and lacking in confidence. Outside the room just before the presentation, they envision themselves as extremely nervous and agitated. They find themselves repeatedly rehearsing in an effort to increase their courage, yet still find that they are extremely anxious. Once they are in front of their audience and making their presentation, they begin to imagine their knees shaking, their hands trembling, their voices quivering and their heads spinning. They see themselves reading through their presentation with a great deal of difficulty. After the formal presentation, they envision themselves fumbling around with the questions posed to them. They find themselves struggling to the point where they are simply unable to answer. After it is all over, they picture themselves walking away from the meeting with their heads down, feeling like complete failures. Furthermore, they overhear colleagues saying that their presentation was poorly organized and inadequately delivered and that the speaker was inferior, inept and second-rate.

If you conjure up images like this, whether in regard to making presentations or any other activity, you would more than likely experience considerable distress and find it difficult to do anything. Rather than carry out a presentation, you would probably want to lock yourself up in your bedroom and stay there! I am not suggesting, however, that it is impossible to deliver a presentation or perform any other function unless you have the appropriate pictures in your mind. What I am suggesting is that if you pay attention to the images in your head, it might be possible to reduce your stress and improve your performance. Employees who complain about extreme anxiety when giving a presentation typically create these types of pictures. So not only are these individuals severely stressed, they also can't do their jobs. In other words, if you visualize yourself crumbling when giving a talk, you may actually do poorly. It becomes a self-fulfilling prophecy. Your actions conform to the pictures in your mind. Certain employees have become experts at picturing the worst. Then they wonder why they're doing so badly. But if we can use our imaginations to hurt ourselves, we can also use them to help.

That is why today, more than ever before, a great deal of emphasis is being placed on the power of the imagination. In baseball, football, tennis and many other professional sports, athletes are being trained by sports psychologists to use their imaginations more effectively. Psychologists are telling athletes that if they prepare themselves properly, using their imaginations, before they perform or compete, they will probably perform more successfully.

You might think that using the imagination in this way is a repetition of positive thinking, but there is a clear difference. Positive thinking involves repeating positive words and phrases to get emotionally charged up in order to perform better. Using your imagination involves not words, but images. A series of performance-enhancing images is used to prepare the body for the real action which is to take place. It is hoped that the performance will be improved, but again there is no guarantee.

To take one example, skiers are encouraged to visualize themselves moving down the slopes just the way they have always wanted to. They are told to picture themselves holding their bodies in comfortable positions, keeping their skis properly angled, taking the hills smoothly, making the turns with ease, generally skiing at their best. After preparing themselves in imagination, they can then attempt to actually ski down the hill. People who are afraid to go down a slope are encouraged to visualize it first. Why? Because it prepares the body for the activity about to take place, and it relieves the anxiety and worry associated with trying something new.

Many Olympic athletes are using their imaginations and are achieving tremendous results. Once, at an indoor track meet, I watched two high-jumpers. Before running down the runway and trying to leap over the bar, each would stand at the foot of the runway for a brief period of time. While they were standing still, I saw their heads in motion as if they were moving along the runway, then coming to the bar, moving over the bar and finally landing. They carried out this exercise three or four times. Only after they completed the exercise imaginatively would they run down the runway for real. These athletes, by the way, were considered to be the two best high-jumpers in the world.

If the imagination is a powerful tool for athletes, it can certainly be useful as a device for employees in the workplace. Let us return to those employees who are troubled by presentations which they may sooner or later be required to deliver. What if they trained themselves to use different images? It should make a significant difference.

Here is what the troubled employees could picture: a couple of days prior to the presentation, they could imagine themselves putting the final touches to the upcoming talk. They could visualize getting excited about the opportunity to lead a presentation about some aspect of their work. The night before the presentation, they could envision rehearsing the talk. They could imagine eating a good breakfast on the morning of the talk. Then they could jump into the car and drive off to work feeling confident that they would do their best. Picturing themselves in the meeting room just before the talk, they could be arranging their notes at the podium and at the same time watching the crowd shuffle in. As they looked out at their audience they could imagine themselves relaxed, comfortable and at ease. Then they could imagine themselves presenting the material in a logical, explicit and entertaining fashion. While carrying out the talk, they could notice that their bodies were relaxed and their minds undisturbed. After the presentation was over, they could visualize themselves handling questions with ease. Regarding those queries which they were unable to answer immediately, they could imagine saying, "I don't know the answer to that, but I will research it and get back to you." After the presentation was over, they could envision themselves leaving the room, feeling good, feeling comfortable and looking forward to their next presentation.

If you visualize these images, you will feel considerably better than if you imagine the set of disturbing pictures described previously. If you are stressed thinking about an upcoming presentation, these images will help to lessen your nervousness. Your imagination is a powerful resource. By visualizing scenes in which you try your best, you train yourself to control your anxiety. So use your imagination regularly. You can resort to it prior to embarking on any activity which you feel troubled about. Picture yourself carrying out the assignment or performing the task just the way you want to. If you rehearse these scenes over and over you will perform more effectively and, at the same, minimize the anxiety that was previously associated with the task.

However, there is a potential trap in all this, and Type As are the ones who usually fall into it. Type As are notorious for thinking that if they imagine things in a certain way, they will work out that way. We must realize, however, that there is no guarantee of this. Visualization is worthwhile, if you realize its limitations as well as its usefulness. If you rehearse scenes in your imagination and picture yourself doing the best job you can, there is a reasonable likelihood that you will carry it out effectively. But there are no guarantees that your experience will be just as you imagined. And if it isn't, you should be prepared to learn from the experience. Most importantly, you can incorporate what you learn into your images, so that the next time you use your imagination, you will visualize a number of new scenes in preparation for an even better effort.

But the key point to remember with this procedure is not to envision yourself performing your tasks perfectly. Perfection is unattainable, so just visualize yourself doing the best job that you can.

This procedure works for athletes because they picture themselves in a reasonable light. Skiers don't imagine themselves going down the slopes perfectly. High-jumpers don't imagine themselves jumping previously undreamed-of heights. They simply visualize themselves doing what they are capable of doing, to get the results they want.

When it comes to activities in the workplace, do the same thing. Imagine yourself performing in such a way that you achieve the results you are after. Once you become really adept at using your imagination in this fashion, you will find that you can accomplish tasks more easily, and also feel considerably better.

There is another way to use your imagination. This method involves talking to yourself in a reasonable fashion while visualizing certain troubling images.

Let us return again to those employees who are bothered about doing presentations. With this approach, you picture that which you are afraid of and worried about. You imagine standing in front of the audience, about to give your talk. You are feeling nervous, jumpy, anxious and stressed. In the midst of this, you ask yourself: "What can I think and say to myself that will reduce my stress, so that I can get on with my presentation?" You then carry on a dialogue with yourself. You might repeat certain questions and answers. For example: "What is the worst thing that can happen to me if I blow this presentation?" "Well, management and my colleagues might not care for this talk." "Where is it carved in stone that I always have to do things perfectly?" "Well, I can only try my best, and if it doesn't work out, I will try to learn from my mistakes." You might continue this self-talk until your level of disturbance is considerably reduced. Once you have rehearsed this sequence a number of times, you will be ready to try the real thing. And you will be less upset when giving the presentation, because you have prepared yourself psychologically.

With this approach, you use your imagination to picture the worst, while at the same time talking your stress away. With the previous method, you used your imagination to visualize helpful images. Which method is better? Try both, and use the method that works best for you.

The main thing is to use your imagination more effectively. Can you picture the results you would get, with a sensible approach to your career and your workplace, combined with a productive imagination? Wow!

From Thinking to Doing

Up to this point, we have been talking mainly about the influence thinking and imagination have on the creation and reduction of stress. But your actions are also important. Typically, people who are experiencing stress end up mismanaging their lives. Employees who are stressed simply do not perform well. Stress interferes with their daily routine and ultimately hampers their careers.

Given that our thinking has changed, and we are now using our imaginations to our advantage, the next step is to consider doing something different. If we are mismanaging our working lives, then it is time to figure out how we can perform more effectively.

1. Asserting Yourself

The first thing to do is to assert yourself. Type As know nothing about assertiveness. They either get very angry, aggressive and hostile, or they withdraw, run away and complain about their terrible work environment. Assertion is quite unlike aggression. Aggression usually involves shouting, yelling, desk pounding, and using the classic word "you," as in: "You cause all my problems," "You are a pain in the neck," "You are no good," "You never do things right," "You are always in the way," and so on. If you keep using the word "you" in every expression, you will either drive your colleagues away, or they will react aggressively toward you. And, if you are trying to work as a team, if you are trying to cooperate with others in the workplace, you are going to have problems.

The two key ingredients are, first, the words you use and, second, your willingness to negotiate with the other person. Rather than prefacing every sentence with "you," use "I": "*I* believe this," "*I* think that," "*I* would like to try this," and so on. What you then add to your "I" communications are the closing statements such as: "What do you think?" "What do you believe?" "What would you suggest?" "What would you like to try?" and so on. When you begin your statements with "I" it becomes very-difficult for the person you are dealing with to construe your discourse as being aggressive. You are simply stating your thinking, your beliefs and your feelings, and then inquiring about the other person's views. In that way, you invite the other person to express his feelings and thoughts. You are not trying to overpower or attack your colleague; you are simply trying to work out your differences with him.

2. Negotiating

Your willingness to negotiate is another matter. This is not only a matter of the words you use; it is a guiding principle. Once you adopt a bias toward negotiation, you need no longer see your colleagues as a threat or your supervisor as an enemy. Instead, you will view these people as members of the same company who, in their own way, are trying to fulfill their responsibilities. Occasionally, differences of opinion, differences in approach, differences in goals, arise. This is the time for negotiation, not aggression!

There is a trap here, too. Type As typically believe that, if they are assertive, they will get what they want. There is no guarantee of this. You can easily start to think that because you have learned to be self-expressive, everything will come your way. Colleagues will be nice to you. Management will be considerate toward you. You will get everything you ever wanted to get from your job. Of course, this is unrealistic and unreasonable. It is important simply to express yourself, whether you get what you want or not. It is important to take the time and the energy to put on the table that which is bothering you. Even if the people whom you work with do not listen to you, at least you have been able to get it out in the open. Stress often relates to people's inability to convey their feelings and thoughts, and what is bugging them. If you get into the habit of self-expression, at least you will know that you tried. That in itself is tremendously valuable.

You should find that once you become assertive, more people will cooperate with you. You should find it considerably easier to work with others. And, very important, especially for the Type A, people will seem to respect what you have to say more often.

3. Communicating

Assertiveness also serves to establish grounds for effective communication. This means that it is important not only to express yourself, but also to listen, share with and support the other person. This may seem very foreign to the traditional Type A. Remember, she has no time for other people. The Type A is the only person who knows what she is doing, and believes that it's a waste of time to talk to others. She simply has to get on with work. But it is critically important to engage your colleagues and managers in a regular dialogue. In many workplaces, the chief complaint among employees is that there is too little communication. That is not to say that people do not know how to communicate with others. The problem more often is the unwillingness of people to set aside time to talk and share. For the Type A, unfortunately, this is practically impossible.

Make it a personal goal to interrupt your working day with a few communication pauses. When the opportunity arises, take advantage of it. This doesn't mean that your entire working day should be spent chattering to the person beside you. But a number of brief exchanges can go a long way. By all means, talk about how you are doing, but, equally important, pay attention when the other person tells you how she is doing.

Once you become adept at engaging others in dialogue, you will be known as a person with good "people skills." Such recognition can be useful. The person who is successful today possesses not only solid technical skills, but also solid communication skills. So you're not wasting your time by communicating; you are investing in your career!

4. Problem Solving

It is useful, too, to work on your problem-solving skills. This may sound simplistic. Doesn't everyone naturally know how to solve problems? But it is not enough just to naturally know. Today, more than ever before, corporations are acknowledging the importance of specific problem-solving skills, and are attempting to ensure that their employees acquire and apply them to their everyday tasks. These skills basically involve: identifying problems, breaking them down into specific challenges, generating a variety of potential solutions, evaluating the solutions, determining the best solution and implementing it. There are many variations on this basic approach. If you are uncertain about your natural ability to solve problems, or think that you could use some retraining, there are many programs available. As with any course you take, however, make certain that you shop around for a reputable program and trainer. Don't be surprised if your manager comes up to you one day and asks you if you would like to enroll in a company-sponsored program. More often than not, you will be expected to participate. Remember, every organization is looking for an "edge." Effective problem solving may be exactly what they—and you—need.

5. Risk Taking

This is the age of the entrepreneur and the "intrapreneur" (who is an entrepreneur inside the organization). Both have in common one characteristic: the ability to take risks. Whether this means taking risks with particular projects, or taking risks with particular people, the same basic principles apply. They can be summarized as follows. To take chances successfully:

- Do not be afraid of failing.
- Do not demand perfection.
- Do not demand guarantees.

Type As typically don't take chances. Type As want guarantees. They want to know that everything is going to work out. They want to know that people are going to treat them well. They want certainties in life.

Instead of uncertainty, the successful risk taker sees opportunity, adventure, experiment, an event which poses a challenge to his traditional way of doing things. This, for him, makes the workplace exciting. However, certain employees never take risks. They are the sorts of people who base their lives on strict predictability and security. But when their expectations are not met, they drive themselves nutty and experience stress, because they won't take a chance!

Taking risks also includes experimenting with new ways of doing things. The risk taker is willing to consider new forms of expression, namely self-expression and assertion, or new methods of problem solving. She's willing to take the chance that her experiments may fail. She may talk to people as she has never talked to them before. She may deal with her manager as she never has before. She will attempt to break down old routines that contributed to her stressful pattern of behavior.

So, try something new, something different, without knowing if it will work out. If you never take a risk, sooner or later you will kick yourself for not having tried!

Risk takers are also willing to be embarrassed. This is one of the most difficult things for Type As. To fail, to be unproductive, to be disapproved of, not to be accepted by colleagues—all these outcomes may give rise to embarrassment. Unless you are prepared to chance embarrassment, it will be very difficult to take risks.

If you do happen to fall flat on your face, and are embarrassed, then what? Type As tend to feel that the world has ended. But it hasn't. How long does the uneasiness last—a lifetime? Of course not. It is temporary. But if you are controlled by your discomfort, it will be virtually impossible to do anything different. Only if you are not dominated by your fear of embarrassment are you free to experiment in life.

In order to confront your discomfort, it can be fun and interesting to purposely create embarrassing situations for yourself. Think of something silly that you did in the past and how uncomfortable it was for you. Do it again! This may sound absurd. But if you can do something that produces embarrassment, and withstand the uneasiness, you will find that you can bear the embarrassment with very little pain. Then you will no longer be controlled by that fear.

Here are some simple exercises that may help you to deal with embarrassment, and so make it easier for you to take risks. They will cause you some uneasiness, but the consequences will not be so severe as to hurt your stature or career in the company.

Experiment 1: The Elevator Trick

The next time you are riding the elevator in your building, turn around so that your back is facing the door and you are facing the other passengers. Say "Good morning" to them. You may also want to smile. This exercise will prove to be somewhat embarrassing for a number of people, because most people in an elevator stare at the floor or at the numbers which indicate each floor. They rarely look at the other passengers. Enjoy the uneasiness until it dissipates.

Experiment 2: The Illiterate Report

If you are accustomed to reading and rereading reports which you have prepared, in order to correct every single spelling and grammatical error, go out of your way to submit a report without rectifying the mistakes. This is not to say that you should do this for the rest of your career, but do it once with the sole intention of making mistakes and suffering some of the discomfort which arises when they're pointed out to you. Then pay attention to how long the embarrassment lasts.

Experiment 3: Memory Lapses

Another interesting exercise is to purposely forget a colleague's name. Think of someone whom you have befriended and trusted for a considerable length of time, whose name you know as well as your own. Then, the next time you bump into that person, pretend to forget her name, and proceed to ask her what it is. You will find that this makes you feel uncomfortable, but the embarrassment will be temporary.

Experiment 4: The Volunteer Guide

Here is another experiment. After work, if you happen to take a subway, bus or streetcar home, when the vehicle comes to a halt in order to let passengers out, stand up and call out the name of the stop. People may think you're strange. On the other hand, they may appreciate the comic relief. But you know as well as I do that whatever they think about you they will soon forget. Your embarrassment will last only a short time.

Work is boring for some employees because they do things the same way every day. People continue to do things the same way because they are fearful of taking chances. If you start to take more chances, life on the job will be more meaningful and more rewarding.

The One-and-a-half-minute Stress Manager

You may have already heard about the "one-minute manager." So far, I have described a number of stress-management techniques which, taken together, will make it possible for you to effectively reduce your stress. These techniques are the tools which, when used regularly, will give you the capability to be an efficient one-and-a-half-minute stress manager in the workplace.

Once you experience symptoms which you recognize as stress-related, stop doing whatever you are doing. The first step is to be aware of what your body is telling you.

It is time for some peace and quiet. Because you may be feeling anxious, agitated, jumpy or nervous, it is important to relax yourself. Use the particular method which works best for you. You may picture a soothing image, or repeat to yourself certain words or phrases which have a calming effect. You do not need to spend a long time on this. If you have been practicing a specific relaxation technique regularly, you should find that you are able to settle yourself down quite quickly.

Once you are relaxed and have reduced your level of stress and anxiety, you are better able to think clearly. Now you can go on to the next step.

Decide what situation at work you got upset about. Then ask yourself what went on in your head, and what you said to yourself, that got you so upset. In other words, what unreasonable thought did you create which made the situation difficult for you, and made you more stressed than you should have been? The third step, then, is to figure out what unreasonable ideas are floating around in your mind.

Once you have determined what you said to yourself which produced the stress symptoms, challenge those thoughts. Start a mini-debate with yourself. Question your unrealistic and unreasonable thinking. But challenge yourself with some real vigor, and make certain that you come up with something more logical and more sensible. Produce thinking that is tied to reality, not fantasy. This is the fourth step: to carry on a debate with yourself in order to formulate more reasonable thoughts.

Now that you are thinking more clearly and sensibly, you can begin to consider what you are doing that is causing stress. Identify the actions which did not get you what you wanted. In other words, work out what behavior was ineffective. Then be sure to do something else. Try doing the opposite to what you have done in the past. Risk doing something different so that you break an old, ineffective habit, and replace it with new behavior that is more effective and efficient. The fifth step, therefore, is to risk changing your behavior so that you become more competent and get more of the results you are after.

To summarize the five steps toward efficient stress management:

1. *Stop.*
If you're stressed, abandon whatever you're doing.

2. *Relax.*
Your mind must be free of distraction.

3. *Think.*
Identify the unreasonable ideas that precipitated your stress.

4. *Counterthink.*
Challenge your unreasonable ideas. Replace them with ideas that are more realistic.

5. *Risk.*
Break the old habits of behavior. Try something new.

The One-and-a-half-minute Stress Manager

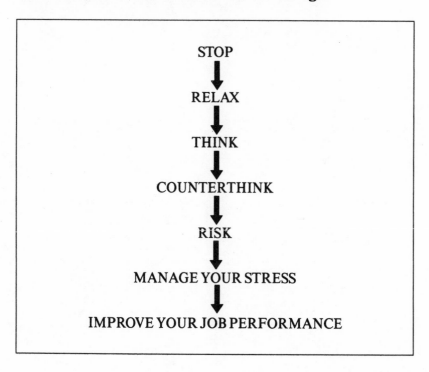

STOP

RELAX

THINK

COUNTERTHINK

RISK

MANAGE YOUR STRESS

IMPROVE YOUR JOB PERFORMANCE

The process of counterthinking is truly an exciting one. It empowers you to challenge illogical, panic-ridden ideas and replace them with more reasonable ones. In a sense, you are developing a personal approach to your emotional well-being. By realizing that stress is linked to your unrealistic thinking and that stress control is connected to your realistic thinking, it becomes possible for you to take charge of your health. You are no longer allowing stress to overcome you; instead you are overcoming it through the process of counterthinking.

II BURNOUT

Defining the Problem

How Do You Know If You Are Burned Out?

There are a number of signs and signals which let you know that you are experiencing burnout. However, the best way to illustrate the problem is to describe an actual life story offered to me by a university professor whom I was counseling.

"I was raised in a really good home. I basically had everything I wanted as I grew up. I had a lot of friends. I remember a lot of happy times. My schooling went reasonably well, so I decided to go on to university. I scored exceptionally high grades in university. As well, I established many friendships and some close relationships. Eventually I graduated with honors. Everyone had a lot of high hopes for me. With my good grades and my family's connections, I was assured of a very attractive career.

"I quickly settled into a meaningful job. I secured an outstanding position at a major university, with the promise that there was a bright future ahead of me. While I was beginning to fulfill some of my career ambitions, I met a wonderful man. I fell madly in love with him. We got married and had two children—a beautiful boy and a darling girl—who fulfilled all of my parental dreams. To complete this apparently ideal family, two dogs were added. So I had my career, the man of my dreams and the children I always wanted. We were like some Hollywood ideal of family life, like the Cleavers on *Leave It to Beaver*.

"Added to this beautiful family were all the traditional trappings. We lived in a large five-bedroom house, had two imported cars in the driveway, wore the most stylish clothing, ate at superb restaurants. In essence, we led the life of an upper-middle-class family. We didn't have the problems which beset many average families—no financial concerns, no marital difficulties, no problems with the kids. You might think that I would be delighted and happy for the rest of my life.

"I should have had absolutely nothing to worry about. But something was missing. Nothing seemed to matter anymore. If a new project came up at work, I was not excited about it. When my kids came home to share their excitement with me, I found it hard to care. I was often exhausted. I simply did not want to work so hard anymore. When I was around my colleagues I was fed up with them. My department head was a pain in the neck. In fact, everyone I worked with was a pain in the neck. I didn't want to be with them anymore. If I could have taken a flight to some deserted island and stayed there for the rest of my life, I would have done it. I wanted to remove myself from all the trials, the tribulations, the responsibilities and the cares which accompany the roles of professor, spouse, parent and so on. I was burned out!"

You might say in reading over this account, "This sure sounds like me at times." In fact, it is safe to say that many people have experienced feelings very similar to the feelings expressed in this story. *Does this mean that everybody is burned out? What does it really mean to be burned out?* The signs and signals include:

- Being irresponsible
- Exhaustion, tiredness
- Being lackadaisical
- Showing little concern for the job and fellow employees
- Anger toward colleagues and supervisors
- Cynicism
- Abdicating responsibility

- Lack of motivation
- Poor appetite
- Disrupted sleep pattern
- Isolation from friends
- Withdrawal from relatives and immediate family
- Quarrelsomeness
- A strong desire to do something extreme and break from tradition
- Depression

Let me share with you a working definition of burnout. Burnout is the depletion of your resources, both physical and psychological, caused by a compulsive desire to achieve, due to exaggerated expectations which you feel must be fulfilled and which are typically, but not always, job-related. Once these are not fulfilled, there is an overwhelming tendency toward cynicism, pessimism and negativity.*

The Depressive Type A
Ask yourself these questions:

Do you find that you are tired and totally exhausted after a day's work, although you are not really overworked?

Do you find it hard to tolerate people at work?

Do you notice that it is difficult putting up with family members and their demands?

Do you lack motivation to get involved in your favorite activities and hobbies?

---

*The idea of burnout was first developed in a classic text entitled *Burnout: How to Beat the High Cost of Success,* by Dr. Herbert Freudenberger. The book is well worth reading.

Do you feel like dispensing with all of your responsibilities?

Do you find yourself complaining more often about how bad you feel?

Does the future look grim to you?

Do you get the strong impression that no one really knows or cares about what you are going through?

Do you find the basics of living, such as eating, sleeping and socializing, not important any more?

Do you get the feeling that if the world stopped turning today you would jump off?

If you answered "yes" to many of these questions, you may be a candidate for burnout.

Burnout versus Stress

The basic difference between burnout and stress is the thinking associated with each. The burnout-prone Type A thinks in very cynical, pessimistic, negative terms. This person is morose and glum and maintains a dreary and dismal outlook. This individual is completely fed up with work and life and has lost the energy and enthusiasm to do anything about it.

On the other hand, the stress-prone Type A thinks in very anxious, worried and aggressive terms. This individual is always fearful that something terrible will occur. At the same time, this person doesn't want others standing in the way of success; otherwise what might happen is their ultimate nightmare—failure. So this individual angrily sets out to work around, work over or work through people.

The Stress-Prone Type A	The Burnout-Prone Type A
Worrisome, fearful, disgruntled thoughts	Cynical, pessimistic thoughts
afflicting the anxious-aggressive Type A	afflicting the depressive Type A
cause agitation, anxiety, anger, annoyance	cause apathy, lethargy, exhaustion
produce stress	produce burnout
resulting in avoidance, indecisiveness, explosiveness, belligerence	resulting in withdrawal, resignation, isolation
leading to heart problems and other physical ailments	leading to depression

From Stress to Burnout

There is no doubt that an anxious-aggressive Type A can become a depressive Type A, by a shift in thinking. Once there is a change from worried, fearful thinking to cynical, negative thinking, and this pessimistic train of thought persists, there is a reasonable likelihood of burnout. Type As make this transition in thought because things aren't working out, success isn't coming fast enough, mistakes are too frequent, people aren't cooperative, management isn't accommodating. When success is delayed, they begin to believe that it will never happen: success will never come their way, people will never listen to them, they will never amount to anything. These Type As have now entered the burnout zone.

I recall a model whom I saw for counseling. She complained about a rash of symptoms which she couldn't explain. She informed me that her symptoms had changed and she couldn't figure out why. She really thought that she was going mad.

Since she had been a little girl, she had always dreamed of becoming a *Vogue* model. She looked after herself; she dressed well; she kept fit and trim. She went to the best modeling schools. She began to get a few small jobs, here and there, but the big breaks weren't coming her way. She began to worry a lot. Maybe she didn't look good enough? Maybe she didn't carry herself well? Maybe she didn't get along with people well? Maybe people didn't like her? Maybe she would never be a *Vogue* model. She always found herself on edge. In fact, she would often blow up at friends and relatives over insignificant things. She picked on people close to her and would even blame them for her misfortune. Then, one day, she woke up and it didn't matter any more. She stopped caring. She believed that she would never make it. Luck was not on her side. She would always be a mediocre, small-time model and nothing more. So she gave up. She stopped pursuing potential opportunities. She stopped seeing close friends. In essence, she had burned out!

The Symptoms of Burnout

Burnout has often been referred to as a sickness of achievers. Burnout typically plagues those with lofty beliefs. It torments those who possess inflated ideas about how the workplace should be, how much they are going to contribute, how fantastic their working relationships are going to turn out and how successful their careers will be. This is not to suggest that having high expectations is a disease worse than death. But when you are committed to lofty expectations, you may have a problem when they do not come to fruition.

Burnout victims typically commit themselves, body and soul, to meeting and fulfilling these extreme hopes. Furthermore, they stubbornly and pigheadedly refuse to lessen their demands, to lower their expectations.

Burnout victims typically demand that their careers offer them more than most careers are designed to deliver. They seem to trust that their work will make their lives far more meaningful, their marriages more enriched, their characters more worthy. But what job can do all this? Burnout victims trap themselves into believing that their careers can make it all happen for them. Typically what happens with these victims is that the payoff from their work is not equivalent to what they dreamt it would be.

Burnout victims lead very restricted lives. The only thing that is important to them is their work. They are compulsively driven to work, to do more and more work, to the exclusion of everything else—people, activities, everything that interferes with their performance and their career. As a result, they are very boring people. If you ever talk to these characters, you will find out that the only thing they talk about is their job, the project they are presently working on or the one they plan to work on. If you discuss anything but their jobs, they tune out, space out and switch off. They simply do not care to listen. You may find these people at parties, social functions, dinners, and so on, always engaged in a discussion about work. If you mention anything about the arts, the sciences, sports, relationships, movies, whatever, they are gone, mind and soul. As soon as you return to the topic of work, they come to life. It is almost as if you plugged them into an electrical outlet and the light in their heads went on again.

Some other features of the burnout victim's personality are noteworthy. Today, women more than men seem to be suffering from burnout. This is a provocative phenomenon, but not really inexplicable. Women, more than ever before, are entering the workplace. They are interested in careers. They are interested in competing. Because of their intense desire to make it, women (like many men) may develop inflated and extreme expectations. Many of these expectations regarding their careers and their contributions to society may be completely unreasonable. When their expectations are not fulfilled, they suffer no less than men in the same situation. Eventually, they experience burnout. This phenomenon affects women returning to the workplace and, most of all, those women entering the workplace for the first time. These novices seem to be most extreme in what they want, what they look forward to and what they anticipate will happen to them. This is not to say that women should not enter the workplace or strive for success. Women, like men, must be in a position to compete and put out their best. But when they set up extremely high expectations and demand uncompromisingly that they be fulfilled, and they are not, burnout becomes a distinct possibility. Another factor affecting women in particular is the very real and continuing domination of many industries by men hostile to women's aspirations. Such barriers are undoubtedly difficult to overcome. If a woman expects and demands that she surmount every hurdle, and fails, she may be in trouble!

Some men, at least, may have become familiar with burnout and benefited from their experience by lowering their demands and toning down their extreme ideas. Other men may have learned from conversation with their male colleagues that they had better get rid of their exaggerated expectations. Such encounters, in individual cases, may have reduced the chances of burnout.

I recall talking to a recent Master of Business Administration (M.B.A.) graduate who, on her first job, was shocked to find "tradition" standing in the way of her progress. She also discovered burnout standing in the way of her health. "I stood top of the class when I graduated from the M.B.A. program. I expected every door to be open when I entered the job market. Sure enough, I landed a job with a top-notch company. My friends warned me that this organization was conservative, but I thought, 'What do they know?' When I was hired, I was told that I would be placed in a high-potential group with other M.B.A. grads. We were all keeners. We worked like animals and loved it.

"Although I was the only woman in the group, I believed that it didn't matter. But my manager regularly reminded me how lucky I was to hold a position which had always been held by a man in the past. But I knew that I was doing well. In fact, I outperformed my five male colleagues. I knew it, and management knew it. Yet when a promotion came up, to my amazement, one of the other members of the group got it. I was furious. I ran in and confronted the manager. He was blunt. He said that I would have to be more patient because the company wasn't used to having such a high-powered woman around who demanded so much, so soon. He also said that I would be promoted, but that it would take a little bit longer. I couldn't believe my ears. I thought this kind of nonsensical thinking went out with the horse and buggy. This was the first time I'd ever experienced discrimination disguised as tradition. I knew all about the laws surrounding discrimination. But it wasn't so clear-cut, because the manager claimed that my colleague deserved the promotion. But I deserved it more. I wanted that promotion and that's all there was to it. The company had no right to obstruct me this way.

"I began to get down on myself and everyone I worked with. I became very angry, cynical and withdrawn. I didn't feel like facing anyone at work anymore. I even began to stay away from work. In essence, I became a burnout statistic. Fortunately, I had some close friends point out that I had gone too far. They spent an entire weekend with me, repeatedly telling me that I couldn't change the world overnight. Also, they told me that I was hurting myself. If my health was important to me, I would need to be more constructive. So I continued to work at the company, although I eventually left for a better position."

Younger people seem to be experiencing burnout more than older people. And this makes sense. Think about some of the younger employees who have entered the workplace. They may be people who have come straight out of school. They may be men and women who excelled in university, were accustomed to good grades and were told that they were outstanding scholars. They come into the organization prepared to set the world on fire. In essence, they expect to be superstars. When their grandiose notions are not fulfilled they become disillusioned and frequently burn out.

Older employees are typically more experienced, have been with the company longer, and are wiser. They are wiser not in the sense that they are more intelligent, but in that they may have been disillusioned. They have realized that it is important not to be so demanding. Because of this realization, they tolerate unfulfillment more easily. They don't drive themselves nutty, or experience burnout as frequently.

Some young people these days jump from job to job, hoping that they are going to come across the perfect position. Why? Because, their extreme ambitions and aspirations are not satisfied as soon as they expected. They are constantly frustrated. They are scrambling around with desperate yearning for the perfect position, the one they always dreamed about. Are these people wasting their energies? Are they going to be in a constant state of unfulfillment? Certain employees do, indeed, devote their lives to a search for something they may never find. This journey of disillusionment is sad, because a lot of energy is squandered and a lot of talent is lost.

Divorced and single individuals seem to be burning out more than married people. The explanation for this seems to be that people on their own often specialize in work, and only work.

After a divorce, people often jump into work with both feet. This behavior is legitimate, certainly, if you don't get carried away. But some divorced people continue to work day in and day out. The more they work, the more they expect from work. Because their marriages were not satisfactory, they expect to get all their satisfaction from work. Every personal failure, every personal inadequacy, will be overridden by the success which they will have to derive from their careers. So they begin to establish lofty and exaggerated aspirations which they must fulfill in order to be compensated for the rotten lives they led with their partners. Through their careers, they must make some kind of a contribution to society. Since they wasted their lives in marriage, they will now make it up through their work.

No doubt it is important to spend time in a meaningful way, especially if you have just been through a divorce. Work and productivity give one a sense of accomplishment. Individuals take pride in doing a good job. But doing a good job can never heal the pain and the wounds that people experience after a divorce. No career can actually eliminate the personal concerns, reservations and uncertainties about future relationships that develop. Work alone can never guarantee that an individual will be regarded as an outstanding member of society. No career is likely to turn an individual into a better human being.

Still, there are those who firmly believe that their careers will keep them sane. And when, in fact, their fantasies and personal demands are not realized, then they begin to set themselves up for eventual burnout. Remember, work is not designed to turn your life around. Work is not designed to correct your relationship problems. Work is not designed to make you a better human being. Work is exciting and meaningful, but it has its limitations. It is not your entire life. If you act as if it is, and you carry with you a whole variety of bizarre and extreme expectations which must be satisfied, you are in deep trouble.

Some single people are also outlandish in their approach to work. Like many divorced individuals, they spend a considerable amount of time and energy on the job, expect miraculous outcomes from their work and inevitably run into trouble. The ones who run into the most difficulty, however, are those who find it especially difficult to form close relationships. These individuals jump into their work as if it is a last resort. Work must give them all the happiness, glamor, glory and success which the rest of their lives have not been able to provide. Once they walk into the workplace with these attitudes, they are in for a big and unpleasant surprise.

Married individuals are less likely to suffer from burnout than divorced or single people. There might be all sorts of explanations to account for this difference. But basically their expectations, especially those related to work, may be more moderate and less demanding.

Married people are more likely to be occupied by other interests and activities. Inasmuch as that is the case, they may not be placing as much emphasis on the job and what the job must do for them. Because they may have more reasonable expectations of their work and career, they are less likely to experience serious problems. Of course, not all married people are shielded from burnout; there are some who have extreme expectations not only about work, but also about their families. They have exaggerated expectations about their marital relationships and how happy they must be, about their children and how bright and well-adjusted they have to be, about their pets and how many tricks they must perform, and so on. When married people get this wound up, they may end up suffering from "double burnout": burnout on the job and burnout at home.

The Burnout Treadmill

The burnout treadmill begins with our value system. Our values, our principles, our standards, the ideas which matter to us, obviously influence our behavior. And our behavior determines the likelihood that we will end up on the burnout treadmill. There are two key influences which have a direct or an indirect impact on our value system: society and the family.

Social Values

What does society tell us? What sort of ideals does society reinforce? What are the subtle messages which society offers to us, which we in turn assimilate?

In no uncertain terms, Western society has tended to make it clear over the generations that we, as individuals coming into the workplace, must rise above our parents. If our parents achieved a certain level of success in their careers, we must surpass them. After all, is this not what progress is all about?

As well, each and every day of our lives, we must work extremely hard. As we work to achieve excellence in the workplace, so will we gain the respect of our community. Being successful in our careers is critically important.

As we continue in our drive toward excellence, we must acquire prestige, status and security. If we accomplish all this, then we will truly be happy and content.

Society has had an even greater influence on us since the onset of television. Television has taught the members of our society to go after the good life. We are all now in the "Pepsi generation," so we have to go after everything, and go after it today, not tomorrow. We've got to have everything now, because who knows? We may not be around tomorrow.

Education and affluence have taught us to reject the simple ways of doing things in favor of more complicated ways and more complicated lifestyles. We must have the best clothes. We must have two cars in the driveway, both imported. We must have a big house. We must have everything that is available—a VCR, a compact disc recorder, a personal computer, phones in the cars. Who knows? If you really work hard, you may eventually have your own satellite in the sky!

But if you do not achieve excellence and success, you may end up with only a few toys. Your life will be too simple. So you will have to push much harder if you really want to enjoy yourself and be truly happy.

Society has also made it abundantly clear to us that we are in the midst of a sexual revolution. Today we must be sexual gymnasts who experience and produce multiple orgasms. If you have only one orgasm while making love, then you can probably consider yourself a mediocre lover. You should try harder to make lovemaking as interesting and as complicated as you possibly can. Because isn't that what lovemaking is all about? You have to become the greatest lover ever. Only then will you be truly happy in your relationships.

Furthermore, we have been led to believe that all relationships must be filled with romance and happiness. If our marriage is not overflowing with romance and happiness, then it may be time for a divorce. In fact, some experts in the field of marriage and divorce tell us that in the future, maybe even in the near future, we will go through a series of marriages, all based on contracts. Prior to getting married, you will sit down with your partner and negotiate a contract. The contract might state that after five years have passed, the marriage is "null and void" unless both parties wish to negotiate another contract. In other words, after the five years have expired, you and your partner will once again sit down and decide the fate of your relationship. If you look your partner in the eye and feel like running away, you will terminate your contractual marriage and go on to the next. And this process might be repeated five, six, seven times during a lifetime. (This is not so far from reality: there are many couples getting married today only after they have negotiated a marriage contract.)

Today, in order to excel as we must, many people feel that it is important to put out a 150 percent effort, even a 200 percent effort, maybe even a 500 percent effort, and—why the heck not?—even a 1,000 percent effort. In other words, we must work twice, three times, four times as hard. Good examples of this mentality occur when professional athletes are being interviewed after an important game. The reporter points the microphone at the athlete and asks: "You had a great game today. How did you do it?" The athlete solemnly replies: "Well, today I went ahead and I put out a 1,000 percent effort on that field. I really did it. I pushed myself beyond my limits and I just simply got it all together. I was superhuman today!"

Viewers watching the interview might say to themselves: "Gosh! I haven't even tapped my potential yet. Look at that athlete, how much he put out. He put out 1,000 percent and was fantastic on the field. Maybe I can stretch myself and go beyond my full potential. Maybe I can put out 1,000 percent and be just as successful as he is." Once, putting out your best simply meant putting out 100 percent. Now, however, the message is: "Go beyond your limits, go beyond your potential, go into that realm of the 1,000 percent."

Not surprisingly, when people who are accustomed to putting out 100 percent strive for 1,000 percent and don't reach their goals, they join the ranks of the burnout generation!

After you have attempted all the above, after you have driven yourself to distraction in the process, you may be too exhausted to enjoy anything. In this state of lethargy, you may end up experiencing the "Peggy Lee syndrome." If you have ever heard Peggy Lee sing the song "Is That All There Is?" you will know what I am getting at. When you are too exhausted to enjoy anyone or anything, you may ask yourself: *"Gosh! Is that all there is to life?"* After you have tried desperately to get all the possessions you should have, after you have stretched yourself beyond your limits, after you have worked maniacally to beat the competition into submission, and driven yourself crazy in the process, you may scratch your head in wonderment. You may finally sit down and ask yourself: *"Was it all worth it?"* And some people get depressed when they realize that it wasn't.

I recall talking with a publishing executive who "wanted it all." "I promised myself and my family that we would have everything we ever dreamed of. I began to work three times as hard as before. If I worked really hard, I knew the returns would eventually come. I was doing well, but not well enough to have the two Mercedes Benzes, the 5,000-square-foot home with a four-car garage on an acre of prime land, the servants, the indoor swimming pool and the trips each quarter to exotic places around the world. So I pushed myself even harder. In the process, I virtually forgot about my children and my wife. I abandoned my friends. I was driven to fulfill my promise at all costs. But the results were still not commensurate with my efforts. I started to drink excessively. I started to take tranquilizers. Eventually, I got extremely depressed, yet I didn't know why. My family and I finally sat down one memorable evening and asked ourselves what we had done with our lives. The plain facts were revealing and devastating."

Family Values

Not only is society influential in shaping our value system; so is the family.

Your family tells you, in no uncertain terms, that in order to succeed, you have to pull yourself up by your bootstraps and get on with it. In the process, be sure that you trust no one but yourself. It is a mean, cruel, wicked world out there, and all the people in it are out for themselves. Therefore, the only person in whom you should have faith is yourself.

In essence, we have been taught to be paranoid, to always be looking over our shoulders to make certain that no one stabs us in the back.

Families also point out that it is important that we persevere at all costs. Never accept defeat. If we suffer a setback, we must overcome it and move on to the final goal: success.

Equally important is to make sure that we never admit weakness to our colleagues, managers or supervisors. If people know about your weaknesses, they will surely take advantage of you. So keep all your feelings and thoughts to yourself. Make certain that you project a positive image at all times. Make sure that you are in complete control, and that no one really knows you. This will guarantee your success.

Families also make it clear that the worst thing we can ever do is let them down. If we happen to fail, we carry not only the guilt of personal failure on our shoulders, but also family-inflicted guilt. No wonder worried employees pace the company halls!

Finally, families have drawn up the eleventh commandment. This commandment is "Do the right thing." And what is the right thing? The right thing is to succeed. The wrong thing is to fail.

In describing the influence of society and family on our value system, I may have overstated and embellished the case. But these standards, principles and values do permeate our lives. They affect our conduct every day. They have a powerful influence which we need to recognize. They are the reason so many people are so unsettled and frustrated at work. Anyone would be flustered and unnerved if they had to live up to these standards. And this, in the extreme, is what burnout is all about!

Definition of Burnout

Burning out is a process of progressive emotional deterioration. It can be roughly described as a process consisting of four phases. In reading the description, you might think that in order to burn out, you have to go through this succession of levels or stages. This is not the case. You don't have to start in Phase 1 and progress to Phase 4. Some people, depending on how distorted and unfulfilled their demands and expectations are, can experience the fourth and most severe level almost immediately. However, I present the process in phases to demonstrate how burnout can develop in seriousness and intensity. Clearly, it is important to identify the symptoms and to intervene as early as possible, in order to halt the course of burnout. Otherwise, the problem becomes more severe and requires more time and greater effort to work out.

Picture Mary, a bright, enterprising, excited law graduate who is ready to start work. It may be her first job or a new job that she is looking forward to. Mary is ready to go. But in addition to her enthusiasm, she has many values buried in her mind which will shape what she expects from the job. They will also determine how she behaves on the job.

Phase 1: The Eager Beaver

Mary enters the workplace and begins to experience Phase 1, the "eager-beaver" stage. Mary, who is loaded with hustle, spiritedness and ambition, says to herself things like: "I must handle everything," "This job must do it all for me," "I have to make this world a better place," "I must overcome and conquer all," "I must be a true success," "I must achieve excellence." In short, her thinking is grandiose. She is overly zealous. She is too idealistic with respect to what she is going to accomplish. So we see a very single-minded and purposeful individual who is bound and determined to succeed at all costs. This person is consumed by energy, drive and a tremendous appetite for glory.

Phase 2: Disillusion

As time goes on, so does the unfulfillment of exaggerated demands and expectations. Mary then drifts into Phase 2, disillusionment. She is beginning to realize that the job simply is not measuring up. It is not satisfying her expectations. However, she knows where the answer lies—in good, hard work. If only she works longer and harder, every-thing will be fine. Although she is disoriented and confused, and at the same time impatient, she knows she must push on. She knows that she must put out more than 100 percent, 200 percent or 500 percent—maybe even 1,000 percent! While she is scrambling around to overcome her disillusionment, she is irritable and has lost some of her confidence, but she is still consumed by the burning desire to overcome adversity, and excel.

Phase 3: Frustration

As time and unfulfillment continue, Mary eventually drifts into Phase 3, frustration. Now she realizes that the job may never measure up. So she becomes more desperate, angry and short-tempered. She begins to blame others for her misfortune. Throughout this stage, she is becoming more and more exhausted. She is losing her enthusiasm for the job. At the same time, she is becoming more cynical and callous. She is withdrawing more and more from colleagues and management. Attendance at important meetings is the last thing on her mind. As she moves through this stage of frustration, she loses more and more confidence. Gradually, she realizes that the job is not going to work out.

Phase 4: Despair

As time and unfulfillment maintain their steady course, Mary eventually drifts into Phase 4, despair. Now she knows that everything is over. Her expectations and dreams will never be realized. There is a tremendous sense of failure, apathy, dishonor and disgrace. Isolation, loneliness, helplessness and hopelessness are the order of the day. She is simply drowning in a pool of misery. When she wakes up in the morning, she feels like pulling the sheets over her head and just staying in bed for the rest of her life. She experiences a tremendous urge to run away and abdicate all responsibility.

If this process continues, Mary will probably end up being severely depressed. The ultimate outcome of burnout is, in fact, a classic state of clinical depression.

During my hospital experience, many patients passed through our mental health services, experiencing the basic signs and symptoms of a depressive disorder. Our team of experts, which included psychiatrists, psychologists, social workers, nurses and occupational therapists, would use their various techniques to assess the person's difficulties. For some people, there seemed to be no problems apparent on the surface of their lives which could explain their depression. They did not seem to have any financial worries. They did not seem to be going through any relationship breakdowns or suffering from any physical ailments. They were not experiencing any major disruptions at work. Everything seemed to be in order.

This baffled and confused us all. There seemed to be no legitimate explanation to account for these patients' depression. Now, as I look back, I think it would be safe to state that these patients were in the later stages of burnout. They had drifted along without paying attention to their extreme demands about work, family and life in general. Because their exaggerated expectations were not being satisfied, these people burned out. Only when things got really bad, and they were feeling extremely depressed, did they finally realize that they needed help from our mental health services.

It is important to know, however, that being burned out does not necessarily mean that you are burned up. Even if you are in the later stages of burnout, you are not necessarily destined to stay there. Strategies to deal with burnout will be detailed in a later section.

Belief Systems and Burnout

Twelve Burnout Myths

Burnout victims usually have very active imaginations. To explain away their problems, they may blame the workplace, their colleagues, their managers and the company itself for their woes and sorrows. It is as if the workplace has done them in, and that is why they are burned out. But burnout is rarely that simple. It is perfectly true that severe changes in the workplace may be associated with burnout. But to go one step further and say that the workplace causes all burnout problems doesn't make sense. Burnout is caused by extreme demands and expectations. These do not originate in the workplace, nor are they created by colleagues, managers or supervisors.

An athlete whom I counseled had a real knack for blaming everyone but himself for a slump he was experiencing, which consequently hurt him much worse in the end. "I knew that I was in a slump, but everyone was always on my case! My coach and manager always asked me how I was doing. They urged me to take extra practice to sharpen my skills. Why didn't they leave me alone? If I wanted extra practice, I'd take it! They didn't have to remind me. Then there was my wife. She would always ask how I was feeling. She knew I was in a slump, so how should I feel? Then the other players wanted to work out with me. Why all of a sudden was I getting all this attention? If people just laid off me, I probably would have gotten out of the slump. But I didn't. So I began to hate people and blamed them even more for my mess. Then one day the manager told me that I had a real attitude problem. It just went from bad to worse!"

That is why I refer to the explanations which burnout victims come up with as myths. I hope in this section to dispel these myths and point out how insufficient they are as causes of burnout. This is not to say that these myths are not significant. But what is more significant are the cravings and demands behind the myths.

The thinking behind these myths may resemble the unreasonable ideas described in the discussion on stress. But these burnout myths are more cynical and pessimistic, whereas the unreasonable ideas were more worried, fretful and fearful in nature. Also keep in mind that these myths lead to withdrawal, isolation and resignation, whereas the unreasonable thoughts result in indecision, avoidance and aggression.

1: Work Overload

The phenomenon of work overload may be very real. There may be tremendous amounts of work to do. But to say that this is the sole cause of burnout is at least questionable.

Burnout victims typically make a number of unique demands which relate to their work overload. If they do not examine these exaggerated beliefs, they will never deal adequately with their burnout. Furthermore, they will not be able to deal with the problem, if it is a problem, of having too much work to do.

The burnout victim tends to reason along the following lines: "There is too much to do, but I have to do it all, and I have to do it perfectly." He feels that he should be able to handle everything. He needs to be in control. If he is not in control, then he thinks: "The heck with everything."

2: Work Underload

Work underload may also be a real phenomenon. If you are a Type A, not having enough work on your plate is a sure sign that you must be failing, that people do not trust you enough, that you are not going to get anywhere in the organization. But whether work underload is a real concern or not, it is important to examine the exaggerated expectations which underlie this particular complaint. What are the unreasonable beliefs that lie behind this myth? They go as follows: "I have to have more work, otherwise it really means that I am a failure." Or: "I should be more productive, more useful, more fully occupied. Because I am not, I will never be able to make progress within the company." Not only do these notions require examination, they also need to be changed before anything else is attempted.

3: Role Ambiguity

Some burnout victims complain that they really don't know what they are supposed to be doing on the job. Because they are so confused, they are burned out. Role ambiguity may in fact be a problem. But whether it is or not doesn't really matter, at least initially. First identify the extreme demands, then pay attention to the other details. The exaggerated beliefs which lie behind this myth may go as follows: "I need my job and I should be treated well. Because I am not being treated with consideration, the heck with it!" Or: "I cannot stand the uncertainty. I cannot stand the confusion about what my job is supposed to consist of. Because I cannot be totally efficient, I will never amount to anything." Clearly, by subscribing to these deeply rooted beliefs, the burnout candidate is setting himself up for major headaches.

4: Inadequate Resources

Burnout victims sometimes believe their mess is caused by a lack of resources with which to perform their jobs. Again, it may be true that there are insufficient personnel to perform all the necessary tasks and activities; the division or department may not have adequate resources. But whether or not resources are an issue, what is really giving grief to the burnout victim are the extreme beliefs which underlie this particular myth. These beliefs may include the following: "They have no right to offer me no help. How will I ever get on the fast track?" Or: "I always have to do everything on my own. I always have to be responsible for everything. I can't stand it anymore."

These notions are the real villains! If work overload, work underload, role ambiguity or inadequate resources truly caused burnout, then every employee who experienced these particular conditions would be burned out. But they are not. There are employees who encounter these same conditions, yet are not as bothered. The people who are burned out are those who hold rigid and uncompromising beliefs about how the workplace should be. And when things don't work out as they should, these same people degrade and debase themselves and the people around them.

5: *Uncooperative Colleagues*

Some burnout victims subscribe to the myth that their burnout is caused by uncooperative colleagues. They may claim: "It's those yo-yos, those turkeys, those misfits whom I have to work with who are ultimately causing my burnout!" Or: "If I was removed from this department or work group, everything would be okay."

You may be working with uncooperative colleagues, or you may not; they are not the cause of your woes. The critical element once again is those improbable beliefs. It is the presumption that other people have no right to be uncooperative, that you are a better person than they, that causes the problems. It is the belief that other people will prevent you from achieving success that leads to burnout.

Let us assume that you are working with uncooperative colleagues. Will these particular expectations and attitudes help you to get along? Of course not. They will produce anger and animosity. Will your anger and aggression make it easier for you to work with them as a team? Not a chance!

Let me digress briefly. In the 1960s, we were told that the best way to deal with anger and aggression was to get it out. We were advised to release all our inner hostility. Once it was discharged, we were assured that we would all feel a lot better and would ultimately be a lot healthier. The trend has continued into the 1970s and 1980s. People let their emotions erupt all over the place. They have been very innovative in finding ways to express their anger. For example, they bought big stuffed toys called "Bobo dolls," took them down to the basement, stuck a picture of the person they hated most, whether it was a colleague or supervisor, on the head of the doll and began to punch it. Other people simply hung up a punching bag in their basement and pounded the heck out of it. Still others purchased "aggression bats." These were sponge bats intended to be used to hit (painlessly) people you felt extremely angry at. Can you picture actually walloping a colleague with your aggression bat? In Japan, some companies have constructed padded rooms. Employees are encouraged to enter these rooms before the workday starts. There, they are supposed to relieve themselves of all their pent-up emotions by screaming, yelling, shouting, punching and kicking. It is assumed that they will then be able to deal with their fellow employees better, and be able to handle their work more effectively.

It is an interesting commentary on the human condition that we resort to all these ridiculous activities in order to get rid of our anger. We are finding out, however, that these activities do not have the desired effect. If you engage in these zany tactics, the only probable result is that you will become an expert at being angry. If you practice any behavior over and over again, you become skilled at it. Imagine being a master of aggression! The danger is that one day you may forget to punch a bag, and instead punch a human being. You might end up swatting a colleague or smacking your supervisor. This is not behavior which is likely to secure advancement for the perpetrator.

Before you express your anger, think. What is going on inside your head that is getting you so worked up? What extreme beliefs are putting you in this position? Once you figure this out and change it, you are more likely to behave in a constructive fashion.

6: Lack of Feedback

Lack of feedback, like the above-mentioned phenomena, may really be an issue, or it may not be. But again, it is not the cause of the victim's burnout. What is important is to identify the unusual beliefs that gave rise to the burnout. These may go as follows: "No one cares about what I do; I must not be worth anything, and I'll never succeed." Or: "I need to be recognized. I need to be told that I am worthwhile. Because no one tells me this, it must mean that I am failing miserably." It is these pessimistic ideas that create the problems.

7: Too Much Supervision

Burnout victims may also ascribe their misfortune to too-close supervision. At the root of this myth is the belief that they are supervised closely because they aren't trusted. They feel that they are being treated like stupid children, and consequently will never get anywhere.

I do not mean to minimize the importance of what goes on in any given corporation. Certainly, there are predicaments, events and situations that are troublesome. I am, however, concerned about employees who always demand that the organization do something, or that the company remedy this or change that. When the changes are not forthcoming, these people become very negative and cynical about themselves and the world around them. I am concerned about employees who do not take charge of their own health and well-being. Once they have solved their own problems, then they can attempt to change things in the organization. The employees who burn out are the ones who get stuck and never get unstuck. They believe that the company has an obligation to eliminate all the wrongs in the workplace, so that they feel better, healthier and more productive. It is this attitude which concerns me!

I counseled a high-school teacher who was convinced that her school should change, so that her needs would be properly satisfied. Not only did the school fail to change, but also other teachers began to see her as a problem. "As a teacher, I have always devoted myself to being the best that I can be. And I guess I expected the same from the school I work at. So I found that after a while I couldn't tolerate the inconsistencies and the mess our department was in. First of all, I had too much work to do. My classrooms were overloaded with students. My responsibilities as assistant head were very unclear. And my department head didn't really trust me. I got so fed up that I demanded that the school and the principal do something. I demanded that corrective action be taken immediately. I went on like this for months. Eventually, I found out that my colleagues saw me as having a chip on my shoulder, and as a troublemaker. But I was serious. And my health was also beginning to suffer. I couldn't eat properly. I couldn't sleep properly. And my friends didn't want to be with me. But worst of all, my teaching was slipping. One day, a close colleague took me aside. She literally shook me. She told me that I can't always have what I want, when I want it. The hardest thing for me to realize was that the system didn't have to change just because I demanded that it should. Although there are very real problems in our department, it takes patience and negotiation to bring about change."

8: *Out-of-date Procedures*

Another myth which burnout victims often believe is that burnout is caused by outdated policies and procedures. Again, this condition may or may not exist. But examine the underlying expectations first. The victims may say, for example: "Why do I always have to put up with stupid policies? I am always the one who has to do things perfectly. I simply can't stand this anymore. I will never achieve excellence this way."

9: Lack of Stimulation

Some people believe that their burnout is caused by lack of stimulation and job enrichment. This is a very significant myth. Type As are notorious for demanding that their jobs be exciting, enriching and stimulating each and every day of their lives. Underlying this demand is the belief that there is nothing interesting outside of work. And if work is not totally and completely enriching, then the victim is doomed to a life of mediocrity.

10: Lack of Recognition

Another myth: burnout is caused by lack of reward and recognition for good work. The underlying belief in this case is that the individual needs to feel that she is good. Indeed, she needs to feel that she is great, that she is doing a fantastic job. If she is not getting recognition for doing a great job, it must mean that she is failing.

11: Job Relocation

A myth that has recently become prominent is that burnout is caused by job relocation. Employees in many organizations and companies are occasionally expected to relocate. Certain employees are asked to take a number of job transfers during the course of their careers. Some do it willingly; others are simply not prepared to move. There may be specific consequences attached to this decision. Employees who refuse to move may not climb the corporate ladder as quickly. They may not always receive rewarding projects to work on. But, essentially, they accept the consequences of their decisions.

There are other employees who do transfer, but blame their relocations for the fact that they are burned out. If you have decided to relocate because of the possible advantages of doing so, and yet blame all your woes and miseries on the fact that you transferred, then there is something grossly wrong. Before you start to fault the organization and the fact that you relocated for your problems, examine your own beliefs. They might be as follows: "I need stability in my life—how dare they do this to me!" Or: "I have to have my roots; it is impossible to go on like this!" If stability and permanence are important to you, why did you take the move in the first place? Presumably you did so in the expectation that certain career advantages would follow. You want to have your cake and eat it too. But because of your unreasonable beliefs, not only will you be miserable, but you will also be unable to enjoy the benefits of relocation.

12: Job Insecurity

The final myth is that burnout is caused by downsizing and job insecurity. This is a very real situation in a number of organizations. Certain companies are undoubtedly going through staff reductions. Some of the survivors may, in fact, feel quite vulnerable. The beliefs that make the situation especially upsetting for burnout candidates are as follows: "I need security." "I need to know exactly what is going on with my career, otherwise I will never get ahead." "I need to be able to plan for the future, otherwise the present is meaningless." These beliefs are killers! No employee today has an absolute guarantee of job security. I am not downplaying the importance of staff reductions and their impact on the employees who are left behind. But you, as an employee, have a choice. You can upset yourself a great deal, or you can learn to deal more effectively with change.

I hope that you now understand and recognize that burnout is chiefly brought on by those expectations and beliefs which are exaggerated and extreme accompanied by thinking which is cynical and pessimistic. That is not to downplay the effects of real organizational conditions and corporate situations. But we cannot necessarily blame our feelings or our burnout symptoms on what the organization is doing to us. We first need to clarify our own expectations and examine what we are saying to ourselves. We need to determine whether we are too demanding and too negative. Once we have done that, it is then possible to look at the company and figure out what problem or problems we wish to address. You'll accomplish far more with this approach!

Burnout and Male Menopause

Many male employees in the workplace have recently decided that the explanation of their burnout is "male menopause." This, for some men, is an extremely convenient explanation, because it seems to simplify their problems and absolve them of all responsibility for their burnout. However, male menopause is a big myth. Not only does it not account for their difficulties; it does not exist.

Supposedly, when a man reaches his forties or fifties, strange biological drives, urges and irregularities occur. He may run into certain emotional problems. He may find himself very unhappy at work, at home or in his relationships. Consequently, he may be driven to do unusual things. He may suddenly quit his job in favor of an activity which is more artistic and spirited in nature. He may take up carpentry, farming or painting pictures. He may become an acolyte of Hare Krishna, join the Moonies or study yoga. Or he may decide to have an affair, often with a woman fifteen or twenty years his junior.

The beauty of this supposed syndrome is that it gives a man an easy way out. In essence, he is no longer answerable for his actions. He can simply say that because he is experiencing male menopause, you have to accept him the way he is. He can do as he pleases. This is utter nonsense!

To blame burnout on male menopause is another major copout. In using this myth, a man says to the company that he is not accountable for what he is feeling, thinking or doing. Nor is he responsible for the changes that need to be made to correct matters. If he goofs at work there is nothing he can do about it. He is being biologically driven to carry on this way. Matters may eventually correct themselves. But those in the workplace, and those at home, will have to be patient and wait.

This line of reasoning and this abdication of responsibility are really part of the burnout syndrome. In fact, if you use male menopause to explain away your burnout, you are simply reinforcing your burnout. You are permitting the burnout symptoms to continue. With the passage of time, the symptoms will either stay the same or, more likely, get worse.

It is important to understand that menopause in men is not a physiological condition, as it is in women. There are no unusual drives or urges which occur in the male when he enters his forties or fifties. In essence, the myth of male menopause involves an abundance of exaggerated expectations which have been unfulfilled. It is the accumulation of one's frustrations, irritations, annoyances and anger with the workplace and the world. It entails disenchantment with yourself and the people around you.

Burnout and Mid-life Crisis

As human beings and employees, we'll resort to any explanation that will excuse us from being responsible for our burnout.

Today, "mid-life crisis" is probably the single most popular label used to account for the miseries of the world. It is more common than male menopause because it affects both men and women. This phenomenon supposedly occurs during our mid-forties. It is that moment of truth, that climax, when we come to grips with who we are, what we have and have not accomplished, what we have done with our careers and our families, and the fact that we are vulnerable and destructible. Certain people are so unhappy with what they discover that they stay in a crisis indefinitely.

Employees who are unhappy at work, who are struggling desperately and are burned out, are sometimes quick to blame mid-life crisis for their condition. They are often convinced that their mid-life crisis will escalate until they fall apart and have a nervous breakdown. They are convinced that they will never recover from their breakdowns, and will probably remain vegetables for the rest of their careers.

I hate to disappoint you, but there really is no mid-life crisis. Like male menopause, this so-called syndrome is not a special condition which suddenly appears just because we reach our mid-forties. We can experience crises at any time during our lives. Some people regularly question what they've accomplished and the direction their careers are taking. Such self-examinations are not confined to mid-life, although some people do wait until then to take a good hard look at themselves.

The worst part of this mid-life phenomenon is that employees use it to absolve themselves of the responsibility for their troubles. This is silly. We are responsible for our problems.

What is noteworthy is that this so-called crisis, like many of our troubles which may take place in our twenties, thirties or forties, is once again connected to those extreme beliefs and expectations which we have buried away in our heads. Therefore, let's stop looking for a convenient scapegoat, such as male menopause or mid-life crisis, to explain away our burnout. Instead, let us focus our energies and attention on those treacherous and misguided ideas in our minds which do wreak havoc in our lives.

Putting Out the Fire: Practical Strategies

Cooling Off

As I suggested earlier, the fact that you are burned out does not necessarily mean that you are burned up. The fire can be put out. First —cool off.

All of us have the ability to remove ourselves from a situation and cool off. You have probably done this frequently, or at least on occasion, perhaps without really paying attention to it.

For example, say you are involved in a heated debate with a colleague. Rather than continue this debate, which may end up in a serious argument, you say to your colleague: "Why don't we cool off for a while, and come back to this later?" You simply remove yourself from the situation.

Another example: You may step back and cool off before you buy something extravagant. Say that you drop into a local art gallery, and all of a sudden you come across a painting which knocks your socks off. You can just see it hanging in your favorite room at home. You look at the price tag and are confronted with a figure of $5,000. Before pulling out your chequebook and writing a cheque, you say to yourself: "Wait a minute, maybe I should go and look around some other galleries." In essence, you have stepped back, detached yourself from the situation and reconsidered the matter. It does not mean that you will not buy this particular piece of art. It simply means that you have decided to think about it and decide whether or not you truly wish to purchase this piece.

Or: One evening you are trying to be the model parent, but your child is not cooperating. He has decided to throw a temper tantrum, and is screaming, yelling, kicking the floor and almost throwing up. Rather than smack him, you decide to step back and cool off. You go into your bedroom and get away from it all. This is, in effect, a time-out procedure. Once you have settled down and reconsidered the situation, you can return and deal with your child in a more composed and even-tempered manner.

So cooling off basically means that you step back and distance yourself from the problem, in order to reexamine your options. It is difficult, while in the midst of chaos, a dilemma or a conflict, to think clearly; this method affords you the opportunity.

I recall talking to a real estate executive who had an intriguing way of distancing herself and cooling off. "When, occasionally, I got into a serious debate with a client or colleague, I would remove myself from the exchange by stating that I wanted to think about things for a short time, and that I would get back to the individual soon. Then I locked myself away in a quiet room, usually my office. Sitting down, I would close my eyes and imagine myself as a third party, watching these two people engaged in a heated exchange. As an onlooker, I tried to figure out what I would do to improve matters, so that the disagreement could be resolved. As soon as I was able to come up with a reasonable solution, I opened my eyes and called up the other person. I'm not saying that this technique is easy. But with practice, I was able to master it. Ultimately, I could get away from any heated debate. I especially tried to remove myself from those disagreements which might possibly lose business for me."

Taking a Close Look at Yourself

A very important strategy when it comes to burnout is self-awareness or self-assessment. It is useful to determine just how upset and distraught you really are. In essence, this means sitting down and taking an inventory of your thoughts and feelings, and figuring out how much you are really suffering. This can be done with a series of questions. If most of the answers suggest that your career and life in general are not too satisfying, then you can assume that you are on your way to being burned out.

Your Cynicism Quotient

Rate yourself on how you typically react to each of the questions described below. Then total up your score and read the appropriate description.

4 = always   **3** = frequently   **2** = sometimes   **1** = never

_____ (1) *Has work lost its appeal and attraction?*

_____ (2) *Is work draining?*

_____ (3) *Do you find your energy sapped after work?*

_____ (4) *Are you no longer enthusiastic about your work?*

_____ (5) *Are you cynical about the way you are being treated at work?*

_____ (6) *Are you preoccupied with what would happen to you if you lost your job?*

_____ (7) *Does your job seem meaningless to you right now?*

_____ (8) *Do you force yourself to do routine things at work?*

_____ (9) *Are your colleagues, even management, goofing off all the time and not pulling their weight?*

_____ (10) *Is your department, your division or your entire organization a maze of red tape and foul-ups?*

_____ (11) *Do you constantly want to be somewhere else rather than at work?*

_____ (12) *Do you find that your friends and colleagues are no longer as enjoyable to be with?*

_____ (13) *Do you feel yourself drifting away from your family and relatives?*

_____ (14) *Do you look for more dangerous diversions and activities to bring excitement into your life?*

_____ (15) *Do you feel resigned rather than enthusiastic about your future?*

_____ **TOTAL**

15–30   You struggle at times with your job and those you work with.
31–45   Your level of cynicism is reaching risky proportions.
46–60   You have a high level of cynicism, defeatism and negativity; if it persists you may find yourself burning out.

These scores and descriptions are not designed to label you or scare you, but to draw your attention to what is going on. It is critical to be aware of your thoughts and feelings. Awareness must precede the motivation to change. The more you realize how unhappy and unfulfilled you are, the more you may be inspired to make some changes in your life.

Ten Steps to Counterthinking

Distorted beliefs and exaggerated expectations are the most critical ingredients in burnout. Changing those beliefs is fundamental if burnout is to be avoided. By changing them I mean reducing their intensity and diminishing their extreme and demanding properties, so that they become more sensible. This does not necessarily mean that you give up your beliefs and expectations. It means that you transform them into something more reasonable and logical. Once you do this, you will begin to establish a "detached concern" for your organization, department or work group. You will develop a concern that finally has limits to it. It will still be important for you to be involved in and committed to your job, but only go so far.

Such limits are valuable, because if you are too consumed by extreme demands you don't perform as well. I'm sure that you have all seen instances in which someone has tried so hard to achieve a particular result that the exact opposite happened. Athletes are notorious for this. Some become so concerned about getting a hit, scoring a goal, catching a pass or sinking a putt that they blow it. Most athletes learn eventually that they cannot afford to take things too seriously or be too demanding; otherwise their performance suffers rather than improves. They learn to try their best, nothing more.

As employees, then, it is important to develop the same outlook, the same frame of mind. To do this, you need to alter your beliefs and expectations, so as to minimize their demanding properties, and finally to gain control over and reverse the process of burnout.

1: Open Admission

A critical first step is to admit that you are burned out. This sounds like a very simple matter, but it is not. Many burnout victims will not reveal their problems to anyone. Many Type As who are burned out will not take on the responsibility of even conceding to themselves, let alone others, that they are in fact burned out. But in making the admission, you clearly demonstrate to yourself and to other key people that you are experiencing problems. When you have stopped fighting the fact that you are burned out, you can start to do something about it.

Let me give you another example in which open admission of a particular problem is necessary to the rehabilitation process: alcoholism. We know that there are many employees who are affected by alcoholism. Organizations have become very sensitive to this problem. One of the most important steps to recovery is for the alcoholic to admit that he or she is an alcoholic. In fact, it is one of the guiding rules of Alcoholics Anonymous. AA makes it clear to its members that it is very, very important to announce to yourself and the people around you that you are, in fact, an alcoholic. Once you have accomplished this, you are on the road to recovery.

Yet another example relates to those who are overweight. If you have ever been involved in a structured weight-loss program, you will know that one of the first steps to losing weight is to admit that you are overweight. If you deny the fact that you have a weight problem, then you are not motivated to do anything about it. Only if your motivation is strong will you be able to lose weight.

Admitting their problem works for alcoholics and for people who are attempting to lose weight, and it can also work for burnout victims. It will work because you are not running away from the problem any more. You are prepared to face burnout head-on.

2: *Taking Responsibility*

The next step is to declare that you created the problem. Burnout victims, as we have seen, are notorious for blaming everybody around them for their own troubles. Type As are the first to state that their colleagues, management and company messed up their careers and made them miserable. If you adopt this perspective, you will have to wait until "they" decide to make things better for you. If "they" don't make things better, you're out of luck. Doesn't it make more sense to acknowledge that you created the problem of burnout? Then the onus is on you to do something about it.

You can manage your difficulties. Why leave it in the hands of someone else? The one thing which most burnout victims fear is loss of control. As they are burning out, they convince themselves that they are losing the power to run their own lives. That power is never lost, but it can be used to develop unreasonable beliefs and expectations. Now you can use this control to develop more sensible ideas. Once you stop blaming the workplace and the rest of society for your woes, you will finally come to grips with your own problem of burnout. It is very exciting to know that you can do something about your own difficulties. You can take charge of the direction which your career will take. You can be the person responsible for changing things, so that burnout no longer plays a role in your life.

3: Self-acceptance

Next, do not condemn yourself for being burned out. Burnout victims are notoriously hard on themselves. By condemning yourself you simply escalate your burnout symptoms. So why make matters worse? Why magnify your problem? Why not accept the fact that you are burned out and go on from there? Being self-critical serves no useful purpose. Besides, if you are depressed, will thinking negative and cynical thoughts make it easier for you? Are you looking for a life of constant self-criticism? You can stop it. And it is important to stop it, because if you are caught up in feeling sorry for yourself, you may have no energy, vitality or effort left for constructive change.

Incidentally, discomfort, hurt and pain are part and parcel of being burned out. They are also part of the process of change. Burnout victims are convinced that once they start to feel pain and emotional hurt, these feelings will escalate, that they will be psychologically ripped apart, will never recover and will remain vegetables for the rest of their careers. Pain is certainly unpleasant, but it does not signal the end of the world. If the burnout victim is convinced that hurt is equivalent to ruination, he will probably be deterred from striving to change his life. So it is important to realize that we are not so fragile, that we will not burst at the seams, as we make adjustments in our lives. Remember the expression, "There is no gain without pain."

4: Challenge

Next, it is important that burnout victims challenge their low frustration tolerance. Burnout victims are notorious for believing that they cannot tolerate anything. They wake up in the morning and say that they cannot endure getting out of bed, putting their clothes on, having to rush out of the house, or driving to work. They cannot face their colleagues. They cannot stomach dealing with management. They cannot endure having to go to meetings. They cannot tolerate having to face deadlines. They cannot swallow having to answer the phone. They really believe that they cannot withstand anything, anymore. They are at their lowest point of tolerance. They are about to crack; they may even have a nervous breakdown.

In fact, there is no such thing as a "nervous breakdown." Nerves just don't break down! People can certainly give up the will to carry on, but nerves do not come apart and stop working. Human beings are fairly resilient. As human beings, we can tolerate quite a bit of frustration. We all know of people who have gone through very serious changes, traumas or crises in their lives and have still managed to endure. We know of colleagues, friends and relatives who have been through a variety of "pressure cookers" in their careers, and were able to tolerate the frustration and disappointment which occurred. We can probably think of experiences we ourselves have been through and have withstood reasonably well.

Therefore, even if you are burned out, you don't necessarily have to give up. It is important to remind yourself regularly that you can endure far more than you usually give yourself credit for.

5: A New Philosophy

Next, it is important that burnout victims change their philosophical approach and adopt a philosophy of uncertainty. Burnout victims are notorious for craving certainty. They want to know for certain that things are going to get better. They want to know for certain that they are going to be successful again. They want to be reassured that they are going to overcome their burnout. They want to know for sure that they are going to be valued again by their colleagues and managers. They want a lot of guarantees.

But what do we know for certain? What can we really predict? We are surrounded by so many changes each and every day. How can we demand that events occur in a specific way, at a specific time? Is it sensible to be upset when events don't unfold just the way we believe they should? But some people do this to themselves. And when their demands are frustrated, they are ready to predict the end of their careers. Giving up this notion makes living a lot easier.

6: *Reduction of Needs*

Next, it is important that burnout victims dedicate themselves to reducing their necessities and conditions for living. We know that burnout victims have a long list of requirements. They have to have two cars, designer clothing, a big house, a personal computer, and so on. They have to have an excellent job, make a fantastic salary, occupy a phenomenal office—the list of necessities goes on and on. If these were necessary conditions to sustain life on this earth, there would not be many survivors. In fact, there are many employees who go in to work each and every day to an environment which is not ideal by any stretch of the imagination. They may not have the biggest office, or make the most money. They might not get promotions regularly. They might not have the latest toys. Yet they maintain a good level of productivity, are reasonably content and retain a sense of humor.

I would like to emphasize again that I am not suggesting that you shy away from putting your best foot forward. But if your list of necessary conditions is too long, you are causing yourself a great deal of hardship and pressure, and burnout is just around the corner. In order to lessen your turmoil, try to realize that what you demand might be better stated in terms of what you "prefer" or what you "would like." What you prefer, you can certainly strive for. But if you make a demand, and your demand is not satisfied, then you are demoralizing yourself. So continue to put out your best effort. Perform to your capabilities. And perhaps you will get most of what you would like to get.

Sooner or later, burnout victims have to discover that their conditions for living are not really essential at all. They are simply one definition of what life could be. We now know that if you define your life according to a variety of extreme beliefs and exaggerated expectations, you will often experience resentment, bitterness, hardship and possible burnout. On the other hand, if your ideas are not extreme and exaggerated, you can roll with the punches. You can ride the ups and downs of developing your career. Many a successful executive has stated that employees who do well are not those who handle the ups in their careers, but those who manage the downs.

As part of the reduction of needs, burnout victims would be wise to consider eliminating their tremendous need for success. This notion may be quite controversial. Let me explain why. Burnout victims maintain that their lives must be filled with prosperity, accomplishment and attainment. If their cup is not overflowing, they will surely be buried in the depths of mediocrity forever. Burnout victims seem to believe that they need success and achievement just as they need food and drink, to survive. But if you approach accomplishment and good fortune in this way, you are asking for trouble. Should you not satisfy these so-called basic needs, you would "die" psychologically, just as you would die physically if you deprived yourself of food and drink. No wonder burnout victims have trouble turning themselves around! Their views of success and achievement are completely and grossly distorted.

Another very important corollary to this idea is to get rid of the idea that only job success gives meaning to your life. Burnout victims are wholeheartedly committed to achieving success at all costs. Even in the latter stages of burnout, they continue to beat themselves into the ground, pursuing the elusive pot of gold at the end of the rainbow. They believe that if they can just get that one shred of job success, it will turn their career around for them. It is almost as if triumph on the job is the only thing that will keep them going.

Now isn't this a bit extreme? Why should job success be the only thing that gives meaning to life? We as human beings can be fulfilled in many ways. We can enjoy our familial relationships. We can derive satisfaction from our social relationships. We can gain joy from our spiritual involvements. We can derive happiness from religious observance. We can obtain pleasure from our leisure activities. We can follow through on a variety of pursuits that are very gratifying.

What is very interesting is that if we gain considerable fulfillment from our outside activities, we end up doing better on the job, because we come to work in a much better state of mind. We come to work not necessarily demanding that we be successful, but with the intention of doing the best we can. If we are not as impressive as we would like to be today, we say to ourselves that there is always tomorrow.

The fewer demands we place on our work and careers, the less pressure we feel, and the less frustration we encounter. We therefore end up performing far more satisfactorily. So if you give up the notion that only job success gives meaning to your life, then you will probably experience more job success. Isn't this motivation enough to change your exaggerated expectations?

7: *Reject Perfectionism*

Next, it is important to be anti-perfectionistic. This injunction would truly burn up a burnout victim! Burnout victims dedicate their lives to perfection. Typically, they believe that if they try a little bit harder to finish that perfect project, to write that perfect proposal, to give that perfect presentation, then and only then will their burnout symptoms disappear. It is almost as if the solution to all of their problems is to be infallible. After all, society values perfection, families value perfection, so these victims believe that they must do the same. What other answer is there to their misery but the glorious pursuit of precision and exactitude?

But we have found that if you dedicate yourself to perfection, you will achieve the exact opposite. Isn't that a crazy contradiction? If you are compelled to pursue that incomparable state of exactitude, you will probably not succeed, because none of us knows what perfection truly is. What is ideal for one person may not be ideal for another. What may excite a colleague may not turn on your manager. Perhaps your manager's definition of perfection should be yours. But what if you do not agree

135

with your manager's definition? What if your manager is replaced by another manager? What if your manager changes her mind about what is and is not perfect? Do you see how silly the whole notion of perfectionism really is?

So why not convince yourself that perfectionism is not worth pursuing? Instead, believe that you will do your best. And if your best is not good enough, at least you have tried. If you are able to maintain this attitude consistently, you will find that you are less disturbed, less agitated, and more productive.

8: *Judgment*

Another very important consideration is to make certain not to judge yourself. Burnout victims routinely evaluate themselves. Indeed, they go one step further: they judge themselves very harshly. If you debase yourself, if you degrade yourself, we now know that you will probably end up feeling depressed.

Depression, of course, is the end result of burnout. It occurs because burnout victims specialize in self-deprecation. Burnout victims do not leave themselves alone! They are critical of how they perform on the job. They are critical of how they act at home. They are critical of how they relate in social situations. They are critical of how they do everything in life. They end up despising themselves to the point where they do not even want to be with themselves.

Does that make sense? Is it going to be helpful in any way? Is it going to allow you to deal with your burnout effectively? The burnout victim truly believes that because she has done poorly, she must be no good. Because her performance is inadequate, it follows that she herself is inept and unfit. So she continues to berate herself, and ends up feeling rotten in the process.

The answer is to not judge yourself. If you must judge anything, then rate your achievements. If you have done something well at work, you can say to yourself: "That project turned out fine. I still strive for continued excellence in my work." If your performance was not so

PUTTING OUT THE FIRE

satisfactory, you can say to yourself: "That did not go well. I will make an effort to improve my work in the future." But to reason that because your performance was inadequate, therefore you are inadequate, will lead to one big headache. You'll hate yourself and you'll hate your work. So focus your attention on what you are doing. Try to correct your performance. Leave yourself out of it. A burnout victim might say: "I am my performance. If my performance is rotten, that means I am rotten." This is nonsense. If you have not done well at a particular task, it simply means that you have not done well at a particular task. It has no general implications for you as a human being. You are still a member of the human race!

A corollary to this principle is to ensure that you do not attach your self, your ego or your identity to your achievements. If your ego is associated with your accomplishments, and your achievements don't materialize the way you demand that they should, then what are you left with? Basically you are left with a shattered ego.

If you separate your identity from your achievements, you can examine them objectively. You can assess what you have done well and what you have not done well. Your attention can then be focused on how to correct your failures and meet your objectives. But when you allow your ego to enter into all your activities, you can drive yourself to distraction. Then your energy and attention are focused on yourself rather than on your work. Once you accept the principle that you are who you are regardless of your successes or failures, you have made a major step forward. It will then be possible for you to deal with criticism, rejection and failure. Burnout victims, rejoice in the opportunity to disassociate yourself from what you do! Enjoy your achievements! Correct your failures! Then and only then will you get more out of your career and more out of life. You will certainly find work more rewarding and the workplace more stimulating.

A further corollary to this principle is that you strive to accept yourself, without any conditions or prerequisites. Burnout victims might laugh at this and say: "Isn't that just like a psychologist! You should never accept yourself, because if you do, you will never succeed.

You will never have any motivation or drive. You will settle for mediocrity and never go beyond that."

I'll tell you something interesting. If you can, in your mind, truly accept yourself as you are, without any limitations, think of the energy, drive and inspiration which will be freed up for what you want in your career. You will no longer be bound by who you should be like, how you should talk, how you should act, how you should perform. Burnout victims are constantly comparing themselves to others. They go around saying to themselves that they should be dressing like him, talking like her, socializing like that other person or making presentations like yet another. They go on and on, and never really accept themselves as they are.

As they continue to invest time and energy in comparing themselves with others in the world around them, they never make the changes necessary to get ahead in their careers. If you spend time worrying about yourself and your ego, how will you ever change? Burnout victims don't have an answer to that question. Yet they persist in demanding to be other than what they are. How can you be any different than you are? Once you rid yourself of the notion that you should be like someone else, you will be free to concentrate on any activity that you wish to. Your motivation will be greater, your inspiration will be greater, and you will probably achieve most of what you wish to achieve.

As an aside, let me draw an analogy to one of mankind's major concerns—losing weight. Most people are obsessed about their figures and their weight. That is why diets are so popular. Certain people seem to lose weight more easily than others. These people do not allow their egos or their pride to get entangled with their weight loss. They recognize that they need to shed some pounds. They figure out a plan, then proceed to put that plan into action. They focus their attention on their performance and proceed in a disciplined fashion to reach their target.

But there are other people who let their egos get involved with their weight-loss programs. These are the people who struggle. They struggle because they cannot accept themselves while they are carrying around excess weight. They are always fighting with themselves. They blame themselves for their rotten looks. They compare and contrast themselves to skinny people. They hate the way they look, the way they walk, the way they dress. They hate themselves thoroughly and completely. If you think this way, you will certainly not be motivated to lose weight. The only preoccupation you have is *you*. How *you* are no good, too fat, too stupid for allowing this to happen to your body. If attention is always directed at *you*, it will be next to impossible to concentrate on what you need to do to lose weight. But if you accept yourself, though not necessarily accept what you do with food, all your energy and attention can be focused on the weight loss. Typically, people who can do that also do much better at shedding the pounds.

This example points out why it is so important to accept yourself. Once you do, you can then get on with the task at hand. You can go ahead and do what is required to reach your goals. You will not be distracted or discouraged or hindered by your ego.

It is equally important that you accept others and their idiosyncrasies. Burnout victims find this extremely difficult. They storm around criticizing not only themselves, but especially others. They blame others for their personal failures. They condemn others for their own insecurities. They blame their colleagues and management for all their defeats.

What will continuing in this way really achieve? It certainly will not help you in your daily working relationships. It will fuel your burnout. If burnout victims did not have such high expectations of others, they would probably not malign and denounce people so much. But why do you need to demand so much of others? Why should you expect others to be what you want them to be? Would it not be easier to accept others and their temperaments, idiosyncrasies and mannerisms? A burnout victim might reply: "This is typical of a psychologist. He is telling us to love everybody. He is telling us to keep our mouths shut, to walk about with a big smile on our faces, as if everything was just perfect and wonderful."

I do not suggest this. To allow people their personal styles, their idiosyncrasies and their dispositions does not necessarily mean that you cannot challenge what they say and do. But challenging people's behavior is not the same as rejecting or disliking the people. If you hate a person, you usually have nothing to do with him, or you fight with him a lot. And the reason you conduct yourself in this destructive fashion is that you expect others to change, to become different because you want them to be different, to do what you want them to do. Wouldn't it be wiser to accept them as they are? They are their own unique selves. Don't pay attention to their egos or personalities; simply focus on how they behave. If you disagree with their behavior, you can challenge it. Wouldn't you then find it more enjoyable coming to work each day? You might even have a good time working with your colleagues. You might even get a charge out of working with management. You might even control your burnout problem more effectively.

I can hear the burnout victims saying: "Okay, how will I ever be as competitive? If I accept people, am nice to people, I will end up being a wimp! I will never amount to anything. People will push me around. I will not be tough anymore, and I won't be as successful." This is ridiculous! If you accept others, your energies are freed up to work with people more effectively, and even to compete more effectively.

Let me give you an example. Say a colleague is critical of some of the work you have done. If you have always demanded, in a rigid and uncompromising fashion, that your colleagues respect everything you do, then you would be extremely upset. You would be angry. You would probably not want to have anything to do with her. However, if you accept the fact that she can come across this way if she chooses to, that she is entitled to be critical, it would make work easier for you. It would allow you to focus your attention on the criticisms being offered. You would then be able to figure out whether they were legitimate or not. If the criticisms were legitimate, you could make the necessary changes. You might even go further, and come up with improvements. Being able to solve problems effectively and remain innovative in the process would place you in a highly enviable position. You might now be viewed as a person who could handle criticism, who could come up with solutions even "under fire" and who could compete with the best of them. All this could come about because you allowed yourself to accept others.

Why do you think office politics is so rampant? It is widespread because employees do not accept one another. They go around talking behind one another's backs and hating one another, because of what that person does or says, or the way he or she dresses or carries on. But what if you changed your approach and your outlook? What if you said to yourself, "OK, people can dress the way they want. People can say and do what they choose to. If what they say and do is not appropriate, I can challenge them if I choose to." With these views, do you still think that you would hate your fellow workers? Do you think that you would fight with them as much? Would you avoid them as much? I believe that the answer to all of these questions is an emphatic no!

The key is to separate people from what they say and do. People are who they are. You are who you are. People do not have to be the way you demand. Colleagues, supervisors and managers do not have to conform to your expectations. When something controversial comes up, and you are troubled by it, don't hate and despise the person it's coming from. Take exception to the issue and work it out. Animosity, antagonism and bitterness are a tremendous waste of energy and spirit. Furthermore, such conflict can destroy a department, or even a whole organization. It certainly guarantees that teamwork is out the window. So enjoy the fact that there are human differences in this world. Accept the fact that people are their unique selves. And when there are differences of opinion, differences in approach or basic objectives, challenge those differences and try to work them out. But keep your ego, and the egos of your colleagues, out of it.

9: Inspiration

Another significant realization is that you don't necessarily need motivation and inspiration in order to do your job. Furthermore, you don't have to enjoy something in order to do it. Burnout victims, however, are committed to the irrational belief that they need to be roused, moved and invigorated each and every working day, in order to do something. They need to feel gratification and excitement from everything which they are involved in, otherwise they simply cannot perform. Is this really true?

Do we have to feel this way in order to perform? Of course not. We all know of many instances where friends were not totally inspired by or overjoyed about a particular task, but still did it. Is it reasonable and realistic to demand that you be exhilarated each and every day? But burnout victims demand this of themselves. As well, they demand that the workplace bristle with stimulants. No wonder they find it difficult to do their jobs! They're spending too much time in their vivid fantasy life, dreaming about how things should be.

You might ask, "What if I am never inspired, or motivated, or enjoy anything I do? How will I be able to carry on in my job?" This is a good point. If you, as an employee, are bored, uninterested and indifferent every day at work, it would make good sense not to come in to work. But here is the mess which burnout victims create for themselves. They argue that if they cannot be inspired and stimulated on the job today, then they will never be excited. This is utter nonsense. First, although you may not be motivated today, you can still perform. You are still capable of doing your job, and doing it reasonably well. Second, tomorrow may bring something else. Tomorrow you may feel the exact opposite of what you feel today. But for the burnout victim, it has to happen now. Excitement has to happen today. And furthermore, there must be guarantees that inspiration will occur with regularity. There will be many occasions when we are not inspired to complete certain tasks. But we can still do them with a fair degree of success and gain satisfaction from the fact that we were able to complete them under conditions that were not ideal.

10: Risks

A final point to consider is that you should take risks in other areas of your life. Burnout victims tend to specialize in one area and one area alone: work. I am not saying that considerable time and energy should not be spent on the job, especially if you enjoy it. But burnout victims usually specialize in work for two significant reasons.

First, they consider themselves to be experts in their respective jobs. Because they are experts, they cannot help but succeed, or so they believe. The expectation of success, therefore, motivates them to continue to specialize in work. They are most comfortable on the job. They think they know what is going to happen there. They presume success is going to be their prize. And they take for granted that they are going to get all the accompanying rewards. The second and more important reason burnout victims specialize in work is their fear of failing in other areas of life. That is why they don't socialize, dance, take up hobbies, try sports or do anything else. They fear that their performance may be only average. If they cannot be outstanding at what they do, and get the rewards which come with an outstanding performance, then what is the point of trying? So they don't try to have fun for the sake of having fun. If they cannot be guaranteed success, forget it.

So burnout victims reduce their world to what goes on in the workplace. This is their first home. This is their hiding place. This is the place where they feel wanted and needed. This is where they will ultimately realize all their dreams. But what happens if their dreams are not fulfilled? They burn out.

Isn't it curious that many people, after they retire from work, immediately suffer health problems? Isn't it also peculiar that a few people, soon after they retire, suffer heart attacks? Who is to say exactly what contributed to their ill health and heart problems? But I think it would be safe to say that because these employees placed so much importance on their work, and took little risk elsewhere, it caught up to them. Once retired, they became desperate, fearful, worried, anxious and distressed, and these emotions probably had a considerable effect on their health.

So, burnout victims beware! Take risks in life. There are many payoffs. You may be healthier, especially when you are no longer working, and you will more than likely do a better job when you are working. Once you involve yourself in activities outside of work, you will place fewer demands on your job. You will not expect it to give you everything that you want out of life. You will be able to approach the workplace in a more reasonable and realistic fashion and enjoy what the rest of life has to offer. It will make the workplace a more satisfying environment for you.

A banker whom I counseled eventually came to a conclusion which helped him to overcome his problem almost overnight. "I always expected too much, but worse than that, I demanded that these expectations be met. Perfection was a critical demand. I made it very clear to my staff at work and to my family at home that things better be done right, and done right the first time. Job success was another necessary demand which had to be fulfilled. I placed my work ahead of everything, including my family. I knew that this was the only way to get recognition and advancement. To this day, I'm not sure why my family put up with it. But the only thing that mattered to me was work and more work. All I would ever dream about was greater productivity and greater success. If my demands were not met, for whatever reason, I became a holy tyrant. People were blasted if they did not live up to my expectations. After all, I did not push people any harder than I pushed myself. In fact, I drove myself crazy trying to meet all of the many self-imposed urgencies. If I didn't do everything just so, I would tear the hide off my back with verbal self-abuse.

"One day, my whole world crashed around me. This happened when I was overlooked for what I believed was a major promotion. How could the company do this to me, after all I had done for it? I went into such a depression that I could barely pull myself in to work. I truly was burned out.

"Then it struck me: the company didn't owe me anything. Anyway, they had been very good to me over the years. It was just me. My family had been telling me this for years, but I never had the time or patience to listen. It was these crazy ideas which had possessed me for so long that led to my depression. But now I no longer had to hang on to these demands, nor did I have to act this way. Oh, work would always be important to me, and I would put forth my best effort. But now I would set limits, which I had never done before. It was time to discard these crazy work habits and at the same time enjoy my family and the rest of the world out there. And you know what—I was sure that I would be better on the job!"

In summary, then, considering everything that has been discussed, what are we aiming for? We are aiming for a philosophical shift. If this sounds imposing, it isn't meant to be. It simply means that you take a look at your exaggerated expectations and extreme beliefs and go out of your way to alter them. Counterthink; reduce their exaggerated, cynical and pessimistic qualities. Generate more moderate ideas. Once this is done, living in the workplace becomes considerably easier. And, surprisingly enough, although burnout victims may still doubt this, performance will be as good as, if not better than, it previously was. This also means, and burnout victims may still be shocked by this, that you will be more likely to succeed. So shape what goes on in your head. Change the extreme so that it becomes more moderate. There is a big payoff waiting for you. You are going to feel a lot better, and you are going to perform more capably. And, most important, your burnout will gradually fade away.

At this point, too, you can shed the label "burnout victim." Once you dedicate yourself to taking charge of your career and to managing your work environment more effectively, you are no longer a "victim."

Burnout Prevention

A Social Support System

Communication, talking and dialogue are all similar in that they imply sharing your thoughts and feelings with those who are important to you. People who are burned out invariably isolate themselves. They are ashamed; they are embarrassed; they feel foolish. They believe that they have let themselves down, along with their community, their family, their colleagues and their company. As a result, they keep it all inside. They hope and believe that with the passage of time, everything will get better. That rarely happens.

There is tremendous merit in opening up. Someone who is recovering from burnout may find this very awkward, but the more you experiment, the easier it becomes. You don't have to share your thoughts and feelings with the whole world. You don't have to run up to every colleague in the workplace and say: "I want to talk to you about my feelings and my innermost thoughts." Think about whom you trust, feel close to and feel like opening up to. Talking about burnout is important, both for the open expression of feelings and thoughts, and for the admission to yourself and key people around you that you have a problem. You are facing up to your embarrassment and shame. Finally, you are realizing that there is no value in denying your problem. You can now begin to share what you have experienced, the expectations that have been fulfilled and those that have not, the things that have worked out for you and those that have not. You can finally reveal your disappointments, disillusionments, losses and defeats.

In essence what you have to form is a social support system. We have always assumed that family and relatives are very important in our social support system. What's becoming more commonplace, however, is that colleagues and managers at work are also being included in the social support network. This does not mean that you are going to be indiscriminate about whom you choose to include in your network. You would want to include certain key people in whom you have faith. We are beginning to learn that people who have strong social support systems seem over the long term to suffer less from stress and burnout. In a sense, support networks seem to act as barriers to burnout and burnout-related disorders.

We have always known that there exist in the workplace so-called "underground communication systems." Such systems are referred to as "underground" because they occur only in private surroundings, with considerable secrecy. They involve gatherings of workers and colleagues who quietly carry on closed-door conversations about what is going on in any given department, unit or organization. In a sense, these underground units act as social support networks. What may occur in the future is that these underground networks will surface and social support systems will become an accepted part of any given organization.

It may be happening already. "Quality circles" could be described as very fundamental social support groups. Although they address issues related to problem solving and task completion, they nonetheless deal in basic terms with the frustrations and worries that employees experience, which impede the progress of quality work. If the discussion included a greater emphasis on the employees' feelings and thoughts, it would become a more standard social support group. Obviously you cannot sit around in your place of work and talk about problems, fears, worries, and so on indefinitely. That would not be very productive. Guidelines would be needed to outline how much time would be devoted to a discussion of feelings and how much to an analysis of potential solutions to emotional problems. Otherwise, you would have a "sensitivity group" on your hands, where employees would simply ventilate their feelings and nothing more. Who needs that mess?

As time passes and as companies become more enlightened, these social support groups will become more legitimate entities. With the sharing of feelings and thoughts and the offer of feedback, employees would realize that they are often not alone, that their painful feelings and exaggerated thoughts are not uncommon. The encouragement and support that certain colleagues and managers can give can go a long way to helping a burned-out employee become a productive member of the team once again.

Options, Options, Options

Employees who are burned out believe that there is only one option: to push, drive, work and overtax their bodies and minds. Then they can trample adversity and make a comeback. But we know that the only thing that gets trampled is the employee. Other options do exist, however. Some alternatives are helpful, others are destructive. Certain choices can contribute further to the problem of burnout; others go a long way toward bringing about healthy and positive changes.

What are these options? The first option is a diversion. A diversion is an activity which is designed to divert your attention away from a particular difficulty. It involves virtually no shift whatsoever in your beliefs or expectations. Examples of diversions include a weekend break, athletics, jogging, partying, a trip—any activity which does not directly address your particular concerns. What are the dangers of diversions? You may get so wrapped up in your particular diversion that you deny that you even have a burnout problem. A diversion offers temporary relief from your problems. This temporary relief becomes extremely satisfying and gratifying. It feels great to get away from the hassles of work. It feels so good that you are tempted to do it over and over and over again. The diversion itself begins to supply you with delusions of grandeur. This activity may become so utterly consuming that you look forward to nothing else. It takes on addictive properties, like certain drugs. All of this may sound far-fetched. But, in fact, many people who are burned out have become psychologically addicted to their particular diversion. It gives them a tremendous emotional high, which they want to experience continuously.

I once counseled a building contractor who had suffered a heart attack. Fortunately, he made a quick and complete recovery. I saw him afterwards, and we discussed what had happened. We discovered that he was burned out both at work and at home. His life did not seem to have much meaning. He was also overweight. He was fed up with his career, his home life and himself. He decided to take up jogging. He jogged regularly each and every day. He became so involved with jogging that it almost became a compulsion. At the same time, he made no effort to confront his burnout, preferring to avoid it altogether. As he was jogging, he also began to notice that he was losing more and more weight. This reinforced his belief that he should continue to run regularly. He ran with intensity, with vigor, with determination and, finally, compulsively. Just prior to the heart attack, he began to notice discomfort and pain while he was jogging. His body was telling him to slow down, but he did not pay attention to the signals. He kept on running, obsessed with and controlled by his accomplishments. One day, he suffered a heart attack while jogging.

I am not suggesting that his heart attack was caused by his jogging. There were many factors which probably contributed to it. To begin with, there was apparently a family history of heart problems. He did, however, approach jogging in a very compulsive fashion, to the detriment of everything else in his life. He also chose to disregard the messages which his body was sending him. He opted for the addictive pleasures of jogging, until one day he suffered the consequences.

Variations on this particular story are repeated every day. Individuals are choosing diversions not because they truly enjoy them, but because through them they can escape from their problems. The results, on occasion, are tragic. Burned-out individuals sometimes choose very dangerous diversions, such as skydiving, mountain climbing and race-car driving. You might think that these people just crave some excitement in their lives. That may, in fact, be true. But it is important to ask why these people suddenly choose risky activities when they are trying to cope with burnout.

There are a host of other, less dangerous activities which people who are coping with burnout can choose from. They include sporting activities such as golfing, cycling, swimming, tennis or pumping iron. There is nothing wrong with these activities; they are very healthy. They all involve physical exertion to a greater or lesser degree, which does seem to promote good health. But when they become too absorbing and engulfing, they can become very hazardous to your health. People who are burned out typically resort to these endeavors not for their physical health value, but for their diversion value. They don't have to face up to their problems, but instead get lost in their sports.

Partying constitutes another popular diversion. Some people are always in search of a party. It is almost as if they work in order to party. They are burned out on the job and burned out at home, so there is really nothing left except parties. Where there are parties, there is often booze, and at times drugs are available. Certain people, instead of coming to grips with their burnout, resort to these extreme diversions. But their difficulties usually get worse.

So be careful. Ask yourself why you are engaged in your particular diversion. If it is because you enjoy it, and not because you are running away from something else, then there is little danger. But if you choose this activity because it is an easy way out, because you can forget about your problems temporarily, you are endangering yourself. This activity may become so consuming that, first, you may never work out your burnout problem and, second, you may suffer some serious health problems in the process.

The next option might be described as major introspection. In short, you spend considerable time thinking. You may be examining those beliefs and expectations which are extreme, in an attempt to reshape them so that they are more reasonable. But there is a trap here. Certain employees who are coping with burnout get too caught up in the deliberation process. They become navel-gazers. They spend far too much time and energy pondering, brooding, reflecting and mulling over their problems. In a sense, they are caught up in cerebral jogging. They become so addicted to thinking that they do nothing else. This is almost as dangerous a trap as the previous option. Although introspection may not be as damaging to your physical health, it does not help you to bring about any positive changes in your work life. Introspection simply allows you the opportunity to find out what you are "all about." It allows you a chance to assess what is going on in your head. But beyond that, introspection does not guarantee action. So this option has definite limitations.

The next option, compromise, is a sensible one. The employee who is coping with burnout goes out of his way to spend a portion of his time changing his beliefs and expectations so that these become more reasonable. After that, additional time is spent figuring out how to do things differently. With this option, he has apportioned his time so that some of it is devoted to mind and some is devoted to behavior. How would he go about changing his behavior? In the section on stress, we discussed a variety of behavioral techniques. Those same techniques can be quite useful here as well. They include time management, problem solving, assertiveness and communication. Mounds of books and articles have been written about these particular techniques. As well, many courses offer training in these areas, so I will not elaborate any further on them.

It is to be hoped that once you yourself change you will be in a better position to bring about some changes in your organization. As well, you will be in a better position to create changes in your working relationships with colleagues and management. If you are going out of your way to improve yourself and your working environment, that is beneficial for you and for those whom you work with. So you win, and your organization wins.

The next option is bail-out. People coping with burnout unfortunately resort occasionally to this. Bail-out is very tempting because it has specific short-term benefits. Once you bail out of, or leave, something, you no longer have to deal with it. So certain employees may choose to transfer from a particular department or to quit the organization. They may change jobs on a regular basis. It is not unusual to find them hopping from their first career to a second, then to a third and so on. They never seem to be able to settle down. They always seem driven in the pursuit of ultimate triumph, and if they cannot get it in one environment, they are determined to get it somewhere else. The commitment factor is not there; they are simply committed to bailing out.

In their private lives, some people who are dealing with burnout seem to do the same thing. They are constantly changing relationships, friendships and residences. Their whole life is one big bail-out.

But very little thought goes into the reasons behind this behavior. If you do not sit down and spend some time figuring out why you are bailing out, and what direction your life is taking, you will accomplish very little. There will be no value and no long-term benefits to your behavior. People who jump around too much, without thinking about what they are doing, end up in a similar mess most of the time. They hop from job to job, but the same problems recur. They skip from relationship to relationship, but the same hassles emerge again and again. And throughout these escapades, they still have not fully recovered from the symptoms and pain of burnout. So bail-out is a dangerous ploy.

The final option may be described as total regrouping. This major choice is a very useful one. It is not necessarily worthwhile for all employees, but it certainly is for some. It is useful for people who have attempted to change their working environment but have found that the results are unsatisfactory. The ultimate answer is to leave. Leaving may involve permanently transferring out of your department, or quitting your company and looking for work elsewhere.

This option is different from bail-out. Here, people have spent some time thinking, and they have changed certain beliefs and expectations which are too extreme. Once this is accomplished, they make changes in how they behave, and also try to alter certain aspects of their job which they are unhappy with. These may include job description, reporting relationships, workload, task responsibility, and so on. If the results are unsatisfactory, then a total regrouping is a workable and viable option. Certain employees have been very satisfied with this choice. They recognized that they no longer fit the organization. These people ended up leaving on very reasonable terms. They were satisfied; the organization was satisfied; and they kept in touch. Thus, total regrouping as an option can be very productive, both for the employee and for the company.

You have now had an opportunity to consider a number of choices. It would appear that the options of compromise and total regrouping have the greatest likelihood of producing long-term as well as short-term gains. The other choices—diversion, major introspection and bail-out —are flawed because they keep you from facing up to your problems. So look for the option that will produce the best results for you and experiment with it!

Happiness

There are programs now being offered on the topic of happiness training. Can you believe it—training people to be happy? Does that tell you something about our society? About our workforce?

Let's examine the fundamental principles of this happiness-training course. The key tenets include the following:

- Stop worrying.
- Be yourself.
- Develop positive and optimistic thinking.
- Remain busy and keep more active.
- Spend more time socializing with others.
- Lower your expectations, aspirations and demands.
- Become present-oriented, not future- or past-oriented.

When you examine these principles, they make a lot of sense. Does the presence of such courses mean that too many people today are burning out and therefore require happiness training? Does it mean that we are all a miserable lot and therefore require regeneration? Does it mean that we don't even know what happiness is about and therefore we require some new skills training? Or does it simply mean that we need some upgrading in the way we create our own happiness? Whatever the reason for the creation of happiness training, the fundamental concepts are reasonable and well-advised. These basic guidelines reinforce many of the ideas which have been discussed in this book. So don't be too surprised if you see an advertisement in your local paper for a course being offered on happiness training.

Hardiness

Now that you have gained control over your burnout, what should you strive for? There is a new buzzword: "hardiness." If we can have hardy plants, we can certainly have hardy employees. But what is actually meant by hardiness?

The first principle of hardiness is to commit yourself to thinking, feeling and doing, but not necessarily to succeeding. There is a tremendous difference. The burnout victims of the past were totally and completely committed to succeeding. The new, hardy employee will be dedicated to more thinking, more feeling and more doing, and therefore will likely succeed more often. It makes sense. If you are devoted to understanding yourself better and doing the best job you can, you will probably be more successful in all areas of your life, especially your work.

The second principle of hardiness is to commit yourself to overall happiness, not specifically to glory and grandeur. The burnout victims of the past religiously committed themselves to going after the honor and splendor which could be acquired only through success in the workplace. But the new hardy employee will go after the whole ball of wax. He will be dedicated to achieving overall happiness. This will include activities both within and outside the workplace. The advantage of this approach is that happiness spreads. If you are happy outside the workplace, you bring that joy with you into the workplace. If you are high-spirited inside the workplace, you take that happiness with you outside.

The third guiding principle of hardiness is to pursue challenges in all aspects of your life, not just in one. The burnout victims of the past ran after achievement, which they believed could only be derived from the workplace. But look at all the other challenges and opportunities which they were missing. The hardy employee will be challenged by a wide variety of opportunities both on and off the job. She will find it easier to handle the ups and downs which occur on the job, because of her many outside interests. She will be able to ride the crests of fulfillment when the work is rewarding, and the troughs of non-fulfillment when the work is routine.

A fourth principle of hardiness is to develop a strong support system and not be isolated from everyone and everything. The burnout victims of the past were social isolates. They could not tolerate the embarrassment and shame of failure, so they separated themselves from others. Furthermore, they blamed the world, the workplace, their colleagues and their managers for their woes and their burnout. This meant that they had to remain detached from everyone, because they were so angry at so many people. But we now know that this is not the answer.

The hardy employee will cultivate a strong social network. This support network will include some key colleagues whom he trusts. In this trusting relationship, he will be able to share feelings and thoughts and come away with a better perspective on matters in the workplace. After all, whether we are prepared to admit it or not, we are all social animals. Social relationships are important, especially in the workplace. Once this strong support system is established, the hardy employee will find it easier to maintain a consistently high level of productivity.

The last principle of hardiness is to make certain that there is laughter and humor in your life. The burnout victims of the past were inordinately somber. They were grim about every aspect of their lives, particularly their working lives. After all, when you drive and strive for success, you have to be serious about what you are doing. But is this really true? Of course not. So the hardy employee will make certain that a sufficient quantity of laughter and humor is part of her working day. What she will discover is that her level of productivity will be as good as, if not better than, it ever was.

Humor

Humor and laughter are very important. Humor has the capacity to change your perspective. It involves a new outlook, a transformation in the way that you view things. When you laugh, when you chuckle, when you giggle, when you see the lighter side of a situation, you have altered your attitude and your perception. Because you have changed your mind-set and because you have placed limitations on your seriousness, you can finally declare that situations and events no longer control you. In essence, you can control a situation by choosing how somber you will become in your reaction. By limiting your seriousness, you introduce a more flexible frame of mind that can only enhance performance. Because you are not locked in by your seriousness, you are able to roll with the punches. You are better able to adapt to change. In a sense, you are master of your environment.

Some of you might think that only mediocre employees have a good sense of humor. They don't take things too seriously. They can afford to laugh because they have nothing at stake. Those who are interested in success, however, cannot afford to be humorous. This is utter nonsense.

Did you know, for example, that people with a sense of humor are usually more innovative and more willing to embrace new ideas and opportunities, and that they usually perform far better? They generally achieve their goals and get along well with people. Did you also know that senior or upper-level managers are usually regarded as having the best sense of humor? Maybe one of the core requirements of a senior manager or executive should be a good sense of humor. Maybe it is something worth striving for.

If that doesn't turn you on, maybe this will. It has been suggested that humor and laughter may reduce your susceptibility to physical illness and disease. It is thought that if you have a good sense of humor and laugh regularly, you may be releasing healing hormones which will help you to maintain your health.

Norman Cousins, former editor of *Saturday Review* magazine, had a very serious illness. His health was gradually deteriorating. It was believed by the attending doctors that he would not recover. Mr. Cousins thought to himself, as he was contemplating what to do about his condition, that if negative or harmful emotions can contribute to illness and to one's vulnerability to illness, then more positive or healing emotions should contribute to health and to one's likelihood of recovery. So he started to watch funny films on a regular basis. He watched a variety of comedies and cartoons, and while watching them he laughed, and laughed regularly. As he continued to laugh, he noticed that his health was improving dramatically.

I am not suggesting that his laughter was the only factor which caused his health to improve. But he himself felt that humor and laughter played a large part in his recovery. Today he is teaching at a university medical faculty. He speaks regularly about the important role humor and laughter play in one's well-being.

Is this, then, not reason enough to consider humor and laughter? There are now conferences solely devoted to the power of laughter, play and humor. If you have forgotten about humor and laughter, you might want to go to one of these conferences. In any case, be sure to incorporate humor into your everyday activities. Look in the mirror. If you don't have laughter wrinkles on your face, make certain that you start laughing more regularly.

The One-and-a-half-minute Burnout Manager

If you believe that you are burning out, consider doing the following. First of all, step back from your situation. Cool off. Take an objective look at things.

After you have stepped back, decide quickly how burned out you are, by asking yourself the series of questions which were listed at the beginning of the section on burnout. If you answer "yes" to most of these questions, you have some problems to tackle.

The next step is to examine your beliefs and expectations. Determine which beliefs are extreme and exaggerated and thus are threatening your well-being. Once you have decided which expectations are the culprits, then proceed to reduce their demanding and intense qualities. This will make you feel considerably better.

After you have changed your outlook and perspective, talk to someone you trust. It may simply mean going next door to a close colleague's office, shutting the door behind you and sharing a feeling or thought.

While you are still talking with your colleague, you might consider the options that are available to you. In fact, you could discuss your choices with your colleague.

All of this might take more than one and a half minutes, but who's counting?

Once you have followed these steps, you may find that the fire has been put out.

So take control of your life. Take charge of what happens to you in the workplace. Rejoice in becoming an excellent burnout manager. The key words to remember are: cool off, assess, counterthink, dialogue and select.

The One-and-a-half-minute Burnout Manager

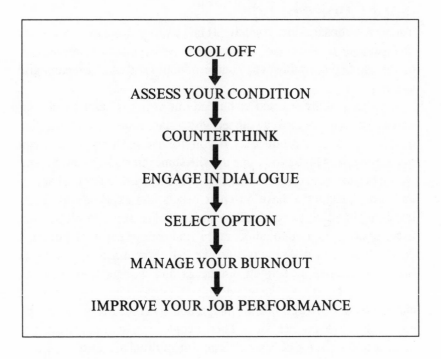

Postscript

Your Choice in Life

You have a choice in life. You have a choice with respect to how you are going to be in the workplace. You can be stressed, you can be burned out, or you can be reasonably happy and productive and enjoy a meaningful career.

Whether you are stressed or burned out or not is basically in your hands. Have you ever asked yourself why certain employees are happier, healthier and more productive? If you are like most employees, you probably have. Maybe you came up with some interesting answers. But we are beginning to discover that employees who are healthier, happier and more productive have different beliefs and expectations. Their minds are filled with a considerable amount of reason, flexibility, tolerance, patience and rationality, and a tremendous sense of humor. I believe that all of us know people like that. Sometimes we marvel at them. Sometimes we scratch our heads and wonder how they can possibly react that way. We wonder how they can work in the midst of chaos, turmoil, disruption and change, and yet come out of the experience with a smile on their faces. These people seem to display a sense of assurance and a sense of peace. It is almost spiritual in nature.

What goes on in your head largely determines how you feel, what you do, how successful you are and whether you are at peace with yourself. What is equally, if not more, exciting is that you can make the choice to think what you wish to, to expect what you wish to and to believe what you wish to. Moreover, you can also change your thinking, your expectations and your beliefs. You can counterthink! If you are unhappy and unproductive at work, you can go inside your head and figure out what is going on. Once you make the necessary changes, you can figure out how to manage your work differently. The results will probably be most rewarding, gratifying and exciting. The events in your life will no longer control you; you will control them.

When you can manage stress and burnout effectively, then you can truly derive pleasure from your career. You can begin to appreciate the challenges you face. You can enjoy the opportunities, the friendships and the unpredictable nature of change. After all, isn't this what life in general, let alone work, is all about?

The Stress- and Burnout-free Corporation

I would be remiss if I did not comment on the organizations and corporations of the future. Those companies which are able to create an environment in which stress and burnout are minimized will likely be more successful, more productive and more likely to achieve their goals than those which ignore these problems.

Today we have been exposed to many management principles, theories and guidelines. We hear that we should value our employees. We hear that employees are our main resource. We hear that we should recognize our employees regularly. We know from the many books, magazine articles and studies on management styles, strategies and the corporate culture that it is critical to develop a workforce, a team of employees, that is committed to productivity and to the success of the organization.

At the same time, we keep hearing that change is all around us. We keep hearing that we must learn to manage change. We must do this because we have moved from the industrial era to the information era.

Today we are overwhelmed by information. We are bombarded by technological advancement which further contributes to information overload.

We have also heard that nations and corporations are moving from an economy which was nation-based to an international, global economy. In other words, we can no longer restrict our planning, production and marketing strategies to our own borders, or even to the borders of neighboring countries. We must now develop a strategy which recognizes the globe as our region of trade.

As well, we are faced with nations which seem to be able to produce various products more efficiently and more economically than we can. There is stiffer competition in the marketplace today than ever before.

As a consequence of all these shifts in our corporate society, it is critical that the workforce be as happy and healthy as possible, in order to face the challenges ahead.

There are still many business leaders and many managers within corporations who believe that employees should leave their problems at home. If you, as an employee, are stressed or burned out, leave it at home. Don't bring your garbage in to work! Just put your nose to the grindstone and keep on producing! This kind of reasoning belongs to an earlier age and should be left in the history books where it belongs.

Today, employees are interested in careers, not jobs. They are interested in the meaningful nature of their work. They are also interested in a variety of other factors which management does not pay sufficient attention to. Employees are interested in knowing that their organizations care. Employees are interested in knowing that their companies are concerned about their welfare. Employees are interested in knowing that their organizations are trying to make the work environment a stimulating and satisfying one. If employees sense that their corporations are putting out, employees themselves will put out. If employees believe that their company is committed to them, the employees commit themselves to the company. If corporations are committed to the health and well-being of their employees, the employees will be committed to the health and well-being of the corporation. Once employees declare their commitment to the health and well-being of their company, you can rest assured that the organization will indeed be healthy, productive and on the leading edge in its field.

In the future, those corporations at the forefront, corporations with a healthy workforce that is prepared to compete, corporations which meet most of their goals and objectives, will have the following in place:

First, companies will make available to their employees the opportunity to have **emotional checkups**, just as we now have physical examinations and checkups. Employees will go to a professional who will systematically assess their Type A behavior, their stress level and their burnout potential. If it is felt after the examination that the employee is experiencing too much of one or the other, it will be recommended that the employee get appropriate help.

Second, companies will have **stress-control centers**, though they might not be called that by name. They might be called counseling centers, holistic health centers or employee assistance programs. Common to these centers will be professionals who will provide help to employees who are experiencing stress, burnout or their related symptoms. In addition to these services, there will be health education and health promotion programs in the workplace. Employees will be taught by professionals how to prevent silly and unreasonable patterns of thought from invading their minds. Furthermore, they will be taught to maintain a course of positive health and "wellness."

Third, organizations will endorse the establishment and maintenance of **support networks** in the workplace. These will be groups—call them "circles" if you wish—that will be devoted to sharing expectations, thoughts, beliefs, values and problem-solving ideas regarding work-related issues. They will be structured with basic goals and objectives in mind. These groups will meet as the need arises. The agenda will typically be geared to helping individuals work through stress and burnout problems which are inhibiting personal productivity.

Fourth, companies will value employees' participation in the various health-related programs and support groups. This will be reflected in their **performance appraisals**. It will be made very clear that overall ratings will take into account their willingness to care for their health and well-being, as well as for their performance.

Fifth, corporations will value **thinking** as much as, if not more than, doing. Organizations will not only ask employees how much they got done, but also how much time they spent thinking about and planning their projects. Employees will be rewarded not just for working harder, but also for working smarter.

Sixth, companies will value **laughter** and a good sense of humor. Employees' presentations will receive better reviews if appropriate humor is incorporated. Through the appraisal process, employees will receive points for maintaining a balanced perspective which incorporates flexibility, tolerance, patience and a keen sense of humor.

Reading this, you might say to yourself, "Come on, now! These are only the wild ramblings of a crazy psychologist! None of this is really feasible, let alone practical or workable. And even if it is practical, who really needs to do this?" Well, corporations that value their workforces will do this. And if you think that these practices are not feasible, you might be surprised to know that they are already in operation! So think and act quickly, because some enlightened organizations are already beating you to the punch!

Bibliography

Type A Behavior

Dembroski, T.M., et al., eds. *Coronary-Prone Behavior.* New York: Springer-Verlag, 1978.

Ellis, A., et al. *How to Raise an Emotionally Healthy, Happy Child.* North Hollywood, California: Wilshire Books, 1966.

Ellis, A. *Anger: How to Live with and without It.* Secaucus, New Jersey: Citadel Press, 1977.

Friedman, M. *Pathogenesis of Coronary Artery Disease.* New York: McGraw-Hill, 1969.

Friedman, M., and R.H. Rosenman. *Type A Behavior and Your Heart.* New York: Knopf, 1974.

Price, V.A. *Type A Behavior Pattern: A Model for Research and Practice.* New York: Academic Press, 1982.

Stress

Beck, A.T. *Cognitive Therapy and the Emotional Disorders.* New York: International University Press, 1976.

Benson, H. *The Relaxation Response.* New York: Avon, 1974.

Christensen, C.M., and L.E. Pass. *A Social Interactional Approach to Counselling/Psychotherapy.* Toronto: OISE Press, 1983.

De Bono, E. *The Use of Lateral Thinking.* New York: Penguin, 1975.

Ellis, A. *Rational-Emotive Psychotherapy*. New York: Institute for Rational-Emotive Therapy, 1963.

———. *The Essence of Rational Psychotherapy: A Comprehensive Approach to Treatment*. New York: Institute for Rational-Emotive Therapy, 1969.

———. *Growth through Reason*. North Hollywood, California: Wilshire Books, 1971.

———. *Executive Leadership: A Rational Approach*. New York: Institute for Rational-Emotive Therapy, 1972.

———. *Humanistic Psychotherapy: The Rational-Emotive Approach*. New York: McGraw-Hill, 1973.

———. *Techniques for Disputing Irrational Beliefs*. New York: Institute for Rational-Emotive Therapy, 1974.

Ellis, A., and R. Harper. *A New Guide to Rational Living*. North Hollywood, California: Wilshire Books, 1975.

Goldberg, L., and S. Breznitz, eds. *Handbook of Stress: Theoretical and Clinical Aspects*. New York: Free Press, 1982.

Kutash, I.L., L.B. Schlesinger, and Associates. *Handbook on Stress and Anxiety*. San Francisco: Jossey-Bass, 1980.

Lange, A.J., and P. Jakubowski. *Responsible Assertive Behavior*. Champaign, Illinois: Research Press, 1976.

Lazarus, R.S. *Psychological Stress and the Coping Process*. New York: McGraw-Hill, 1966.

Lazarus, R.S., and S. Folkman. *Stress, Appraisal and Coping*. New York: Springer, 1984.

Meichenbaum, D., and M.E. Jaremko, eds. *Stress Reduction and Prevention*. New York: Plenum, 1983.

Selye, H. *Stress without Distress*. New York: New American Library, 1975.

———. *The Stress of Life*. New York: McGraw-Hill, 1976.

Wessler, R.A., and R.L. Wessler. *The Principles and Practice of Rational-Emotive Therapy*. San Francisco: Jossey-Bass, 1980.

Burnout

Cherniss, C. *Professional Burnout in Human Service Organizations.* New York: Praeger, 1980.

Cousins, N. *Anatomy of an Illness.* New York: Bantam, 1981.

Edelwich, J., and A. Brodsky. *Burnout: Stages of Disillusionment in the Helping Professions.* New York: Human Sciences Press, 1980.

Ellis, A., and R. Grieger. *Handbook of Rational Emotive Therapy.* New York: Springer, 1977.

Ellis, A., and W. Knaus. *Overcoming Procrastination.* New York: New American Library, 1977.

Ellis, A., and I. Becker. *A Guide to Personal Happiness.* North Hollywood, California: Wilshire Books, 1982.

Ellis, A., and M.E. Bernard, eds. *Clinical Applications of Rational-Emotive Therapy.* New York: Plenum, 1985.

Ellis, A. *Overcoming Resistance: Rational Emotive Therapy with Difficult Clients.* New York: Springer, 1985.

Faber, B.A. *Stress and Burnout in the Human Services Professions.* New York: Pergamon, 1983.

Freudenberger, H.J., and G. Richelson. *Burnout: How to Beat the High Cost of Success.* New York: Bantam, 1981.

Freudenberger, H.J., and G. North. *Women's Burnout: How to Spot It, How to Reverse It, and How to Prevent It.* New York: Doubleday, 1985.

Howard, J., et al. *Rusting Out, Burning Out, Bowing Out: Stress and Survival on the Job.* Toronto: Financial Post/Gage, 1978.

Jones, J., ed. *The Burnout Syndrome.* Park Ridge, Illinois: London House Management Press, 1981.

Lauderdale, M. *Burnout.* New York: University Associates, 1982.

Machlowitz, M. *Workaholics: Living with Them, Working with Them.* Reading, Massachusetts: Addison-Wesley, 1980.

Nowack, K.M. "Who Are the Hardy?" *Training and Development Journal,* May 1986, 116–18.

Pelletier, K.R. *Healthy People in Unhealthy Places*. Monterey, California: Merloyd, Lawrence, 1984.

Pines, A., and E. Aronson. *Burnout: From Tedium to Personal Growth*. New York: Free Press, 1981.

Potter, B. *Beating Job Burnout*. San Francisco: Harbor Publishing, 1980.

Postscript

De Bono, E. *Tactics: The Art and Science of Success*. Boston: Little, Brown, 1984.

Drucker, P. *Innovation and Entrepreneurship*. New York: Harper and Row, 1985.

Kanter, R.M. *The Change Masters*. New York: Simon and Shuster, 1983.

Klarreich, S.H., Francek, J.L., and Moore, C.E. *The Human Resources Management Handbook: Principles and Practice of Employee Assistance Programs*. New York: Praeger, 1985.

Klarreich, S.H. *Health and Fitness in the Workplace: Health Education in Business Organizations*. New York: Praeger, 1987.

Peters, T.J., and R.H. Waterman. *In Search of Excellence*. New York: Harper and Row, 1982.

Tichy, N.M., and M.A. Devanna. *The Transformational Leader*. New York: Wiley, 1986.